Games and *Simulations* in History

DAVID BIRT and JON NICHOL

LONGMAN

LONGMAN GROUP LIMITED
London

*Associated companies, branches and
representatives throughout the world*

© Longman Group Ltd 1975

First published 1975
Second impression 1976
ISBN 0 582 36301 2

Printed in Hong Kong by
The Hong Kong Printing Press Ltd

Contents

For Conel

Decimal conversions for lengths referred to in this book :

1 mile =   1.61 kilometres
1 furlong = 201.25 metres

Preface

Simulation and gaming are becoming increasingly important in the classroom. The technique is already widely used in geography and the social sciences. It is hoped that this book will serve to introduce history teachers to simulation as a teaching aid alongside slides, filmstrips, archive units etc.

The sections of the book outline a variety of aspects of history gaming. The first two chapters relate the technique to developments in history teaching and analyse the types and organisation of simulation activity. Chapters 3–8 contain six different types of history games and simulations, and show the possible range of topics that can be dealt with. Chapter 9 explains how to construct simulations, and chapter 10 deals with practical problems of their use in the classroom.

This book developed out of our experiences with history games over the past three years. During that time we have been supported and encouraged by a large number of individuals and institutions; we are most grateful to these. In particular we would like to thank WPD Murphy, Head of History at the City of Birmingham College of Education, whose enthusiasm helped launch the idea; also BH Tolley of Nottingham University Department of Education who arranged to have our games widely tested; and to our pupils at Repton School, many of whom used their free time to help us improve our games. Our final and greatest debt is to our wives, Deryn and Rosalind, whose patience, consideration and support made this book possible.

DJHB
JDN

1

New Approaches to History

Views of history as a classroom subject

History is under attack as a school subject. While history courses at universities are oversubscribed, the subject is under pressure both from outside and inside the schools. Some academic historians are pessimistic about the value of attempting to teach history in schools at all as an academic subject: Professor Elton would even relegate it to the level of telling stories. There is a widespread feeling that history teaching in schools is a poor preparation for taking the subject at university, as university teachers find that they have to undo much of the damage they consider the schools have perpetrated.

In the schools themselves, history is on the defensive. As a discipline it is under attack from the social sciences, which claim to have superseded its methodology. With 'contemporary relevance' as the watchword, traditional history is criticized as being unconnected with the needs of the pupils and, almost by definition, as being of limited value. Clearly, it is in danger of being relegated to limbo along with the classics. In reaction to this threat, many history courses have become more and more related to the contemporary scene. Increasingly, history is losing its identity as a discipline in a

1

world of 'integrated studies' and 'humanities courses', and seems to be becoming a branch of current affairs.

Behind both lines of attack, there emerges a picture of history teaching as it is thought to exist today. History teachers are suspected of attemping to form pupils in their own image. Their main concern is considered to be the production of apprentice professional historians. In secondary education the emphasis is placed on formal work, note taking and essay writing. It seems that the teacher either lectures or dictates to the class. Syllabuses are regarded as watered-down versions of university courses, with the emphasis being placed on the chronological development of national societies. Discipline is rigidly maintained, with conventional classroom seating arrangements. The history room (if it exists) appears as a sterile environment, often containing little more than the pupils' desks and a blackboard. Such a picture does seem to have some validity: a recent survey of 146 representative Liverpool schools showed that 50 per cent of history classes only occasionally undertook group or individual work, and that in general teaching aids were only rarely used.

In a technologically advanced era, with the pupils being subjected to the attractions of the mass media, history is in danger of being left in the Dark Ages. The traditional goals and methods of history teaching are eminently defensible, but that is not the issue when the subject generally is being undermined. There needs to be some major modification in the classroom approach to the subject. History games and simulations are being presented as an exciting new teaching aid to meet some of the specific criticisms levelled at the way history is at present being taught.

New approaches to history

In the last decade, significant changes have begun to emerge both in the approach to history and its teaching in schools. Three strands have intertwined to produce a diametrically different attitude to the subject. Academic history in the universities has responded to the challenge of the social sciences, particularly sociology, and this is being reflected in history in the schools. Despite the hostility of many professional historians to sociology as a discipline, much of the terminology and many of the ideas of the social scientists have been borrowed and absorbed. History has been given a new cutting edge as a discipline: it stands alongside social studies and complements them by giving them historical depth and perspective. Also, history can be regarded as the test bed for the social scientists. Historical studies increasingly deal with the handling of concepts and conceptual 'models'. This is particularly true of the economic historians. In school teaching the value of a concept-based approach has been recognized by the Schools Council 8-13 Project. Through studying a concept in its historical context, the pupils gain an added dimension to their understanding. In this way history is easily integrated with other disciplines, while existing as a separate area of study.

The second strand has emerged from changing attitudes towards history as a discipline. The traditional approach to history has deepseated nineteenth-century origins. Following Ranke's work on the Continent, and Acton's in England, history developed as an 'objective' study of developing societies or movements, such as liberalism. The emergence of nationalistic histories and the historicist approach of the Marxists reinforced the idea of the historian as an apparently detached observer of the past. While positivism, or the scientific approach to history, is enshrined in historical methodology, it has limited attraction for pupils where it dominates historical studies. In the 1930s, RG Collingwood (following the work of Benedetto Croce) radically revised the positivist view of history. Instead of being regarded as the objective study of a finite body of information, history came to be considered more as a process of interaction between the historian and his evidence. Collingwood saw the historian's role as that of bringing the past to life, attempting to see history through the eyes of those who made it. In relation to the classroom, this places a much greater emphasis on the student handling and evaluating original and printed historical material, and trying to form his own picture of history as it happened.

The final strand of thought which has led to a change in the view of history teaching arose from the work of child psychologists. Although Piaget's conclusions have been questioned, his work still provides a broad framework of reference for the teaching profession. The idea that the child's mind goes through recognizable stages of development has been accepted, and this has direct relevance to

3

history teaching. With many pupils in their early teens still being mainly in the concrete stage of operations and unable to handle abstract ideas meaningfully, traditional teaching methods may require modification. A swing away from generalization is called for: it becomes crucial to face pupils with actual material on which to work. Ideas, even as apparently simple as 'king' or 'revolution', should be presented in direct relation to evidence: the concept of 'king' applied to William I is very different when applied to William IV.

The changes in academic history, the philosophy of history and child psychology have been combined in the conclusion that traditional history teaching should be stood on its head. Instead of history being a body of received information and ideas, it can be viewed more as an activity by the pupil, who learns his history as a voyage of discovery, experiencing historical evidence in a visual, aural and tactile manner. As with traditional history, the pupil is being trained as a historian but with a radically different view of history than previously. Instead of the teacher being a purveyor of information, his role is to aid the pupil to recreate a picture of the past as it happened and as it appears to him. The teacher takes a more passive role: he sketches in the background and provides the framework within which the pupils can handle material. The discovery approach develops social skills, particularly empathy. When used with a lines of development, 'patch' or concepts approach it can be directly related to the contemporary world of the pupil.

The new history in the classroom

If history in schools is accepted as a voyage of discovery, the onus is on the teacher to approach the subject in ways which will facilitate this. The teacher becomes the provider of materials for the pupils to work on. However, the quantity and nature of the materials needed may cause concern to the hardpressed teacher. The scope and use of such materials is capable of 'infinite variety' and is ever expanding. Evidence that the resources boom is already under way is seen in the widespread acceptance of history work cards based on original material at the junior and middle school levels, and the introduction of archive material into the classroom. Source material is used in many forms, both original and printed. 'Jackdaws' have been widely

4

adopted, while Keele, Sheffield and Nottingham universities have all been producing archive units. Also, groups of local teachers are cooperating to prepare archive material for the classroom. To these may be added the filmstrip and slide projector, epidiascope, overhead projector, gramophone, tape recorder and videotape, which are all invaluable in introducing illustrative material. The reading of history plays and documents provides interesting aural evidence, while historical films combine aural and visual material.

All these aids are useful in helping the pupil to build up his own view of the past. History games and simulations provide a teaching method additional to those mentioned above. Simulations both illustrate ideas and present evidence in a manner which impinges directly on the pupil's consciousness. They are a new technique which seems expressly designed to cater for many of the demands of the new history.

History games and simulations

An important aspect of the new history is that the pupils should be able to understand history as it happened. This can be done in two ways. They can take a relatively detached view and build up a complete picture of events as they occurred. An alternative (but complementary) way of entering into the spirit of a past age is to attempt to see events, no matter how complex, through the eyes of contemporaries. Drama is already widely applied to history:

> We then tackled the acting of documents. There are endless possibilities in local history - a meeting of the manor court from the manorial roll, a borough court in action, the churchwarden or the constable at work, a poor-law case. I base a skeleton script on the documents and leave the rest to free acting. The time William the Conqueror's commissioners met the Shire court of Leicestershire and the priest, reeve and six villeins of the village of Scraptoft gave their evidence, while French and English glowered at each other from opposite sides of the court; the clerk was very suspicious of the jury's evidence. It was great fun; Domesday came alive and some of us learned a lot about it. (*History in Schools 8-14,* ed. Joan E Blyth, p. 37. University of Liverpool Institute of Education.)

5

Role-play can take many forms, and it should be applicable as a teaching approach to most historical situations. In history games and simulations, the pupils take the role or roles of characters in history. They are presented with authentic information and have to take decisions similar to those which faced the figures whose roles they are taking. Simulation can tie in closely with traditional teaching approaches, as well as the newer discovery methods. If possible the pupils should be faced with accurate historical information on which to act: this can take the form either of original documents or printed material. Some kind of original material (normally in reproduction) is to be preferred as it brings the pupils into direct contact with the past and makes the role-play more realistic.

History games and simulations can take many forms. They can be created for most age and ability levels, and are particularly effective with the lower ability pupils who may find difficulty with a concepts approach to the subject. The type of game and its degree of complexity can be tailored by the teacher to the pupils' needs. Simulation has the following advantages:

1. *Motivation.* It introduces a positive stimulus into the classroom. By playing out the roles of historical characters and facing the same problems and decisions as figures in history, pupils become highly motivated. The enthusiasm which simulation generates often spills over into other parts of the course.
2. *Empathy.* Role-play helps pupils understand and appreciate points of view different from their own. By associating with the position of figures in history, the pupils are drawn into a form of understanding and an insight into character and motivation which might otherwise be denied them. This makes them more able to understand their fellows.
3. *Insight into the historical process.* Simulation enables the teacher to demonstrate the multiplicity of possible outcomes of any historical situation, and give the pupils a new insight into the working of history. *It thus acts as a powerful antidote to history being regarded as an inevitable series of events which has to be learnt.*
4. *Learning and recall.* As pupils take historical roles, they learn history *from the inside,* since they relate their roles to the

6

simulation's historical framework. The acting-out of roles and the active handling of historical material enables pupils more easily to recall the topic concerned. Recall is helped both by the pupils' identification with the topic and by enhanced understanding, because the pupils have themselves created a realistic historical situation and can thus grasp in their own terms what happened.

5. *Social skills.* Much of history simulation takes place in small groups; it therefore encourages cooperation between pupils. In this it is extremely useful for mixed ability forms, where the more able can help the less able pupil. At the same time *all* pupils are able to contribute to group work: the less able pupils will provide ideas of value, since most simulation exercises are open-ended and have a wide range of 'correct' answers. Verbal skills are also developed because simulation involves the pupils in argument and discussion. Pupils have to justify decisions at all points, so the technique helps to increase vocabulary and fluency in using ideas and information.

6. *Variety.* Simulation introduces a new element into the classroom.

While history simulation has these advantages (some of which are possessed by other teaching techniques), it is not a panacea. The technique is an additional aid, to be used alongside existing methods. Indeed, this is part of its value for it can easily be integrated into existing teaching courses. However, the type of role-play and simulation activity has to be carefully chosen. A class role-play, unless carefully constructed, may cause playing problems if it requires pupils to operate largely independently of the teacher's control. Also, however successful simulation may be, the technique should not be used continuously or it might lead to boredom (as would happen with any other technique). Classroom approaches and problems will be discussed at greater length in Chapter 10.

A further problem may arise in attempting to simulate a unique historical event of which the pupil probably knows the outcome, for instance the Battle of Waterloo. There is also the difficulty of representing men of genius in action, as their behaviour is precisely the kind that cannot be adequately simulated. One solution is to simulate only the opening stages or selected moments in the known event, as is done in *The Russian Revolution* (p. 123).

References

Armstrong, RHR and Taylor, JL (eds). *Instructional Simulation Systems in Higher Education,* Cambridge Institute of Education, 1970.

Ballard, Martin (ed). *New Movements in the Study and Teaching of History,* Temple Smith, 1970.

Burston, WH and Green, CW. *Handbook for History Teachers,* Methuen, 1972.

Carr, EH. *What is History?* Penguin, 1964.

Chorley, RJ and Haggett, P (eds). *Frontiers in Geographical Teaching,* Methuen, 1965.

Collingwood, RG. *The Idea of History,* Oxford University Press, 1946.

Elton, GR. *The Practice of History, Methuen,* 1967.

Lamont, W. *The Realities of Teaching History : Beginnings,* Chatto & Windus, 1972.

Plumb, JH (ed) Crisis in the Humanities, Penguin, 1964.

Sturley, DM. *The Study of History,* Longman, 1972.

2

The Nature of History Games and Simulations

History games and simulations are based on the concept that within any historical situation a framework of factors can be identified. The individuals and groups who operate within that framework can be isolated and their various attributes described. Where the framework is of more general application, a model of the situation can be developed. For example, a simulation could be produced around a model of the establishment and running of a turnpike trust. Already historical frameworks and models are widely used by teachers, even though they may not have rationalized them as such. Many textbooks on eighteenth- and nineteenth-century social history deal with the 'typical' enclosure village and the general impact of the Agricultural Revolution. Historians use more general frameworks when they discuss peace treaties, battles, constitutional movements, nationalism, imperialism etc. Simulation recognizes that in history certain identifiable constraints operate to influence the outcome of a situation.

Simulation gives the two-dimensional historical framework a three-dimensional aspect. The pupil is able to see for himself how history develops by taking the role of an historical character and then acting according to the circumstances which affected that figure. In revealing the historical process, simulation shows the importance of chance factors in giving a twist to the shaping of events. By definition,

9

historical frameworks are open-ended, so simulation enables the pupil to grasp how important the 'Cleopatra's nose' element is in history.

The wide variety of historical frameworks is reflected in the differing types and complexity of history games and simulations. However, it is possible to categorize games and simulations according to the kind of activity involved. The historical framework is the key element in determining the kind of simulation activity. The framework dealing with the planning of a canal route by a surveyor will be markedly different from that which handles a topic such as the French Revolution. A simple rule of thumb is that the younger or less able the child, the simpler the framework should be, and the shorter the historical time span covered. A further factor in categorizing history games and simulations is the type of class organization that is involved.

The organization of history games and simulations

History gaming organization divides into three main types: single role-play, group role-play and class role-play.

Single role-play

Single role-play is where a pupil or group of pupils takes the role of a single character in a historical situation. As the only figure concerned, they have to take decisions in reaction to the changing circumstances which faced that figure in reality. This form of gaming relies on the interaction between the pupils and an unfolding pattern of events. Even with a class of some forty pupils, this means that up to forty different role-play exercises can be occurring round a common situation, though in practice we recommend that pupils where possible work in pairs or small groups.

Much of the value of the single role-play is that it encourages a wide spread of comparative work. Also, this form is useful for illustrating the multiplicity of possible outcomes in an historical situation. In *Village Enclosure* (Ch.6) no two groups reach the same conclusion about the distribution of land among the villagers, yet all the schemes put forward may be equally valid.

Single role-play is easily adapted to introduce a competitive (and

10

perhaps additionally motivating) element into a game. Such competition is sometimes an accurate reflection of the historical situation. In *Ironmaster* (Ch.5) the history of industrial development is being shown through the work of a single firm; each group of pupils represents such a firm and is in competition with other groups. In reality, the iron industry in the eighteenth century developed through competition between a large number of small firms.

Group role-play

The second type of gaming organization is group role-play. Here each pupil in a group takes the role of a different historical character or party, and interacts with other members of that group. Each group is in fact a self-contained playing unit and there is not necessarily any contact between groups.

Group role-play is normal for board games, where interaction within the group can take a competitive turn, showing the importance of conflict in history. It has the advantage that the pupils work in small, manageable groups: it is also a flexible form, allowing one group of pupils to engage in gaming while others pursue different activities.

In group role-play, the pupils absorb information through the rules of the game, chance cards or sheets, and information sheets; on the basis of these they make their decisions. The form is suitable for simulating the behaviour of small numbers of men or groups in an historical situation, for instance during revolutions, peace treaty negotiations, cabinet meetings or royal councils. It is particularly useful for enlivening diplomatic and political history at key points in the syllabus.

Class role-play

Class role-play is the final type of gaming organization. In this, the whole class participates, being divided up into various groups which represent the parties involved in an historical situation. Within each of these groups, individual pupils can be given specific roles. For example, in *The Russian Revolution* members of a group representing the Bolsheviks can take the roles of Lenin, Trotsky, Stalin etc.

Class role-play depends on the interaction between the various groups. After being briefed about the background to the situation,

11

each group is provided with information which is often in the form of news sheets, newspaper accounts, transcripts of broadcasts etc. (tapes of actual broadcasts can be used where available).On the basis of these, each group attempts to make alliances with other groups around an agreed programme. The amount of negotiating can generate a very high level of pupil involvement and motivation. This form of role-play encourages pupils to identify closely with characters in history and to try to understand the complex problems which faced them.

Types of gaming activity

Individual, group and class role-play exercises can take many forms. The different types of role-play activity are shown in the matrix below. Gaming activity covers five main areas: board games, map work, tables, discussion and in/out tray. None of these areas is exclusive and a well-constructed simulation will often contain a number of these elements. Also, most elements are suitable for use with individual, group or class role-play organization.

Simulation matrix

Simulation activity		Class organization		
		Individual	Group	Class
Board game	Reality			
	Abstraction			
Map	Location			
	Development			
	Progression			
Table	Decision			
	Analysis			
	Account			
Discussion	Negotiation			
	Debate			
In/out tray	Linear			
	Complex			

Definitions

The difference between a game and a simulation is related to the accuracy of the historical framework. The simpler and less realistic the framework used, the nearer to gaming: the closer to the historical actuality, the greater the element of simulation.

Board game – reality

A realistic board game is one which represents an actual historical situation. Normally it will take the form of a contemporary map of the period. By following a set of rules, the pupils have to reach a certain goal. Such a game is *Trade and Discovery* (Ch.7) for which the map is based on the work of sixteenth-century cartographers; the rules and chance factors mirror those factors which faced Drake during his circumnavigation. Additional information can be contained in information sheets: pupils can use these to help decide which character to portray, as in *Frontier* (Ch.4).

Board game – abstraction

These board games are constructed on the same lines as commercial games such as 'Monopoly' and 'Snakes and Ladders'. Each square on the board can represent a specific period of time, and the pupils have to reach a goal by moving a certain number of squares each turn. The squares can be dated and marked with chance numbers (or, if large enough, actual chance information occurring in its historical sequence). A board game covering the two years leading up to the passing of the 1832 Reform Bill could be divided up into squares each of which would represent a month. By playing through the game and reaching the final goal of Parliamentary Reform, the pupils can see (through the eyes of the reformers) how the Reform movement developed.

Board games of this type are excellent for junior pupils as they show the simple linear development of a topic. They are also very flexible, being suitable for individual or group role-plays, or for use by individual pupils to play through a sequence of events.

Map game – location

Here the pupil has to choose between different sites, judging each site according to a number of factors. The map should be historically

13

accurate. An example is Part 1 (p.71) of *Ironmaster* where the players choose between five different possible sites for their new iron works. The factors they have to judge each site on are accessibility to iron ore, limestone and charcoal or coal. A location exercise is a convenient way of introducing pupils to the idea of gaming and at the same time conveying information on which the rest of the game may depend.

Map game – development
In this a map is divided up into a number of areas (normally square or hexagonal) which the pupil has progressively to fill in according to the rules. For example, in *Frontier* the pupils represent early settlers in British North America, and the rules, chance sheet and information sheets enable them to understand many of the factors affecting early settlement. Each colonial area is divided up into a number of squares which the pupils have to settle. A similar exercise occurs in Part 3 (p.100) of *Village Enclosure* where the Enclosure Commissioners have to allocate land among the freeholders of the village.

The technique is suited to showing how a situation developed over a period of time. Each area filled in can show the passing of time as well as extension into a region: in *Frontier* the settlement of each square might be said to represent a period of five to ten years. Map development games are suitable for single or group role-plays.

Map game – progression
For this, the pupils are given an outline map or series of maps to fill in. When they have chosen their roles, they have to mark certain features on the map. These features will be sited according to historical information contained in the text and/or on the outline map. A simulation based on map progression is *The Development of the Medieval Town* (Ch.3). Here the pupils take the roles of successive leaders of a settlement from its origins as a Saxon village to the twelfth century, when it becomes a typical medieval town. Map progression here illustrates changes in a situation over a long period of time; it is equally adaptable to short time spans, for instance the results of a single decision such as building a canal or road.

Decision tables
These are used to give a numerical basis for making decisions, and are
14

often combined with another form of gaming activity. A decision table allows careful evaluation of the different points for/against a course of action, and can be used in a wide range of circumstances. In *Ironmaster, Village Enclosure* and *The Development of the Medieval Town* such tables are employed to help determine decisions about different sites; in *Frontier* they aid the pupils in deciding which areas to try to settle; and in *The Russian Revolution* a decision table is used to help pupils decide which seems the most hopeful party to adopt.

Analysis tables

An analysis table works on the same lines as a decision table but it is used to evaluate decisions already taken. Its function is to check the validity of previous decisions and to estimate the basis on which they were made. Such an analysis table occurs in *Village Enclosure* to check on the land allocations of the Enclosure Commissioners. The technique could also be used to check on the acceptability of, say, a peace treaty presented to a group.

Account tables

In games where a competitive element is included, account tables are often useful. They can show the amount of income a player derives from his operations at various stages of the game. Account tables do away with the need for counters, cards, paper money and so on, so they make a game more manageable in the classroom, and yet enable the pupils to simulate the activities of men engaged in a range of commercial transactions. A useful byproduct of using account tables is that the pupils receive training in mathematics and domestic accounting.

Where possible, account tables should be based on historical examples (as is the case in *Ironmaster*). If the account table is fictitious (see *Frontier)* it is best to construct it on a 'unit' as opposed to a monetary basis. The method of using units is fully explained in chapter 9.

Discussion – negotiation

In both group and class role-plays, decision-making between groups of pupils or individuals (representing 'parties' or single characters) can be based on negotiation. On the basis of historical information

15

supplied, pupils can assess their own positions and attempt to make agreements or deals with other players. The possible number of combinations of groups/individuals able to reach such agreements is very large: this makes negotiation a very flexible form of role-play activity. It is also flexible in that the approach can be extended to many historical situations, with the pupils building up a picture of events as the simulation progresses. It is thus a successful way of involving pupils in a complex developing historical situation.

Discussion – debate

A more formal framework for discussion is the debate. In a debate, the various individuals or groups in a class role-play have to declare their position with regard to a proposal or set of proposals. The pupils announce their viewpoints (and the reasons for them) and try to persuade the rest of the class to adopt such viewpoints. When each pupil has expressed his opinions, there is a class vote which resolves the point at issue. In *Village Enclosure* such a point is whether the village shall enclose or not, a decision that could be preceded or followed by negotiation if required.

In/out tray – linear

This form will probably be used for a simulation covering a long period of time. As the simulation progresses, more information is introduced stage by stage, sometimes in the form of 'historical prompts' which return the pupils to the actual historical situation after a decision or series of decisions. An example of this is the beginning of Part 3 of *Village Enclosure*. Alternatively, the intention may be to break up a difficult historical process into small sections to aid comprehension; each section would then introduce a new element or development. The form is thus particularly suitable for lower ability/age levels.

In/out tray – complex

If an involved topic covering a relatively short period of time is being dealt with, this form may be suitable. Here news sheets or 'broadcasts' interrupt a simulation at regular or irregular intervals, and apply to all or only some of the players. The form is thus particularly effective for a topic such as a revolution or the negotiation of a peace treaty, where new developments may completely alter the situation. This process is clearly seen in *The Russian Revolution*.

Simple and compound games

Where only one or two of the above elements are present in a simulation, it may be said to be *simple*. Such a simulation might deal with a single aspect of a topic. For instance, *Turnpike* (shown below) covers only the route of a new road and omits factors such as construction, hiring of labour, wages, repairs and upkeep, financing, tolls trustees etc. which all played a part in the turnpike movement. A simple game is particularly suited to the junior age level: it can be played through quickly, and it does not demand that the pupils carry large amounts of information in their heads.

The Turnpike

Below is a map of a stretch of countryside through which runs a track. The track serves as a road between two villages, marked A and

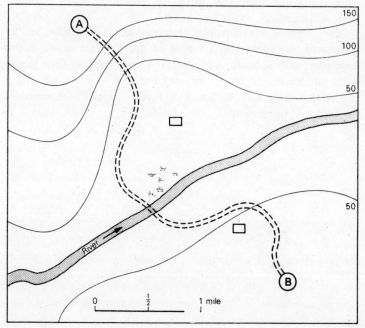

B on the map. A number of local tradesmen and gentlemen who own the land in the neighbourhood have decided to get the track improved. In winter it becomes a sea of mud and its numerous pot-holes are full of water.

They have got a Turnpike Act through Parliament to build a new road between the two villages.

To build the new road the following improvements will be made.
1) The old track will have all sharp bends removed.
2) The track will be re-routed so that it will be easier for carriages to be pulled up steep slopes.
3) Turnpikes will be built at the ends of the new road and where other tracks meet the road.
4) The new road will not pass within half a mile of any large house of the gentry (indicated by squares on the map).
5) A bridge will be built across the river.

Using the map, it is your job to provide the best route for the new road. You must mark in the new road on the map in the right places, showing where the various features of the new Turnpike Road will be sited.

The games and simulations illustrated in chapters 3–8 are all *compound,* i.e. containing a variety of the elements shown in the simulation matrix. Such variety tends to make many of these games more suitable for the secondary level, but there is no reason why a teacher should not select sections (e.g. Parts 1, 2 and 3 of *Ironmaster*) for use with younger pupils.

3

The Development of the Medieval Town

The Development of the Medieval Town is a simulation with role-play elements. It is designed for the eight to fourteen years age range and is suitable for most ability levels.

It aims to show the gradual evolution of a settlement from a Saxon village to a typical twelfth-century walled town. Since the development of the town (illustrated on maps 1 and 2) is guided only by general principles, each pupil's final town will be different. This provides a basis for discussion about why the towns developed differently.

The pupils can work individually or in small groups, and the simulation may take up to six 40-minute periods to complete.

Framework

The game

The pupil takes the role of the leader of a Saxon band which voyages to England about the time of the

Historical actuality

From A.D. 383 onwards, the British appealed to Rome for help against Saxon invaders. With the withdrawal of the Roman legions by 411, the raids breakup of the Roman Empire.

Map 1 shows part of a major river; possible settlement sites are marked.

Having chosen a site on Map 1 the pupil draws in a stockade enclosing one large hut and seven smaller ones.

The next problem is to clear land for farming. Up to 1000 metres of heathland round the settlement can be cleared. The new farmland is drawn on Map 1.

The settlement does not grow for the next five hundred years, owing to difficulties and almost continuous warfare. One of the sites (B) is raided by Vikings, and destroyed.

became increasingly frequent. By the mid-fifth century, Saxons and Frisians were beginning to settle in England.

The early Saxon settlements were grouped round rivers. The Norfolk settlements (on loamy soils) were reached through Yarmouth and up the valleys of the Yare and Wensum. In western Norfolk and Cambridgeshire the distribution of cemeteries indicates that rivers flowing into the Wash (e.g. the Nene and Welland) were used to get to the well-drained gravel sites beyond the Fens.

Saxon villages took a certain standard form. Normally they were dominated by a wooden longhouse, up to 30 metres in length, with smaller huts grouped around, as at Old Yeavering in Northumbria, and St Neots in Huntingdon.

The main form of subsistence was arable farming. In Cambridgeshire land around settlements was cleared, and barley, oats, wheat, flax and woad grown.

The villages were grouped on a tribal basis, and conflict tended to be endemic. During the years from *c.* 500 to 800, out of the mass of warring tribes and factions emerged the three kingdoms of Northumbria, Mercia and Wessex. These kingdoms fought for supremacy and were subject to attacks from Scotland and Wales. There were also further invasions, and by the ninth century the Vikings had emerged as a new disruptive menace. The Vikings sacked Lindisfarne in *c*. 793 and their raids continued to be savage and widespread for the next century.

By 1050 the country has become more settled, and the population of the village is growing. The pupil draws in new huts and a new field formed from clearing woodland. Also, a bridge across the river is indicated.

During the tenth century a *modus vivendi* was worked out between the earlier settlers and the Vikings. Consequently there was a spread of settlements from the more easily farmed soils to the heavier clay lands. The clearance of forest and scrub became widespread.

Also, the bridging of rivers occurred. Many wooden bridges were constructed, such as that at Stamford Bridge and the one over the Thames at London.

The stockade becomes too crowded, and new houses are drawn in outside it.

By the eleventh century population pressure was forcing many villages to expand outside their original boundaries.

New areas needed to be cleared for cultivation. Enclosures of lands were called 'tuns'. Thus the new bridge leads to the possibility of a third field on the far side of the river. This field is drawn in.

The extent of the Saxon enclosures is shown by the survival of the term 'Tun' as a place name. Tunbridge indicates a tun by a bridge.

Tracks which lead to the bridge are shown.

Inter-village commerce both by land and river greatly increased. In later

21

All the above details are now transferred to Map 2.

Anglo-Saxon England a number of ways (roads formed by the passage of traffic) grew as well as streets — artificially-made roads. A portweg was a road leading to a town (e.g. London).

After the Norman Conquest, William I grants the land on Map 2 to one of his knights. The pupil, representing the knight, draws in a motte and bailey castle and a church.

The Norman conquest led to a massive redistribution of land to William's Norman supporters. The extent of this is indicated in the Domesday Book (1086-87). To control these acquisitions motte and bailey castles were built, such as at Shrewsbury.

Under Norman rule the population continues to grow. The tracks become roads, and a quay is built along one bank of the river, with warehouses nearby. Also houses spread onto the far bank of the river. These details are entered approximately on Map 2.

The Norman rulers were willing to derive income from all sources. There was often a connection between town and manorial profits; at Alnmouth the Percy family built a port to serve their family interests.

A terrible civil war breaks out, so the pupil, now taking the role of the Norman baron (grandson of the knight) draws in a stone castle. The townsfolk are also concerned about defence, and appeal to the King for a charter allowing the town to be walled.

The early Norman period of relative stability ended with the outbreak of civil war in 1135. King Stephen (1135-54) seized the throne, but was never able fully to assert his supremacy. He was challenged by the Empress Matilda.

Many towns became fortified during the 'nineteen long winters while Christ and his angels slept' when feudalism became fragmented.

As a baronial adviser to King Stephen, the pupil has to work out if it would be in the interests of the King to sell such a charter.

In the twelfth century, many boroughs acquired 'liberties'. It was probably by such a grant that Stephen managed to keep London loyal to him (apart from one brief lapse) for nearly two decades.

The town gains control over its own commerce, and gradually guilds are formed.

Many towns' charters granted them the right to farm their own taxes, play a role in their internal government, and manage their own markets.

Later the question of walling the town comes up again. There is a class discussion (with each pupil taking the role of a different townsman) about whether the new King should be asked for a charter to wall the town.

Richard I (1189-1199) sold a number of charters in order to raise money for the Third Crusade. He also raised loans from rich townsmen, such as William Cade: this shows the growing importance of towns, largely owing to capital accumulation.

The town aldermen decide to press ahead with a charter application, which is granted. The pupil then has to draw in encircling walls, taking into account factors of economy, defence, existing houses etc.

The town is complete.

By the end of the twelfth century towns had come into their own as centres of trade and finance, with an increasing degree of autonomy.

23

Equipment

Pencils, erasers and tracing paper; compasses would also be useful, if available.

Playing procedure

1. The class should be divided into groups or pairs and a copy of the text given to each pupil.
2. Read Part 1 (below) aloud down to Table 3.1, and check that the pupils understand Map 1 (e.g. that the woodland is *all* wooded).
3. Work through at least two decisions in Table 3.1 with the class, so that pupils fully comprehend the allocating of marks. When the table is completed, the majority decision of the class can be compared with individual decisions.
4. To transfer the 'stockade' to Map 1, tracing paper should be used. The 1000 metre segment for the field is most easily drawn in with compasses.
5. Part 2 begins with the destruction of site B. This is less suitable than Sites A or C for a number of reasons.
6. In Part 3 it must be emphasized that the pupils have to judge the *importance* of the factors from *the point of view of King Stephen.* This section can be run as a class debate, with each baron giving his view.
7. Part 4 is designed to form a framework for a general class discussion. When the pupils have read through the points 1–10 (for/against building town walls), they can select roles from the list of eighteen town characters shown on the Information Sheet. After the characters have been chosen, the pupils should re-examine the general points 1–10 from the viewpoint of their character. A debate follows, in which each character tries to influence the class to accept his/her viewpoint. At the end, a vote can be taken, and the result recorded.
8. The first paragraph of Part 5 is meant to offset any impression that the pupils may have gained that the medieval town was in any way democratic.
9. The finished Map 2 should be compared with Map 1 by each group.
10. Pupils can examine each other's maps and discuss variations in town development and the reasons for these.

The development of the medieval town

Part 1 Early settlement

Around the year A.D. 350 as the power of the Roman Empire declined, a growing number of Saxon tribes (from the area of North Germany) raided the coasts of England. After the Romans had withdrawn their soldiers from Britain, large numbers of Saxons settled in South and East England. Their settlements spread inland up the main rivers such as the Thames and the Trent. This was because the Saxons used ships for transport.

Map 1 shows part of one such river and the surrounding country-side. Imagine that you are at the head of a group of Saxons. You have just sailed and rowed up the river from the east, and decided to found a settlement somewhere in this area. It is important that you should choose the best possible place.

There are a number of things to consider. For defence, the settlement will be surrounded by a stockade (strong fence) and ditch: but it will only be really safe if it is built on a good defensive position. Then the settlement will need to be near farming land and water; and it will also need a supply of timber.

Your followers point out three possible sites (marked A, B and C on Map 1). Look carefully at these sites: a really good site will have the following:

1. *A good defensive position.* Other Saxon bands or raiders may come up the river and attack this area.
2. *Nearness to heathland.* This is the only land it is possible to farm with the light ploughs you brought with you in your ships.
3. *Nearness to the river.* This will provide drink for the settlers and their animals, and water for washing and dyeing clothes.
4. *Nearness to the woodland.* You will need timber for building your huts and the stockade, and also for firewood. The trees are mostly oak, so pigs can also use the woods for feeding (on acorns).
5. *Avoidance of the marsh.* The land near the marsh is waterlogged, which makes it impossible to farm and also unhealthy. The marshes cannot be drained.

Note that it is always difficult to cross the river, and sometimes impossible.

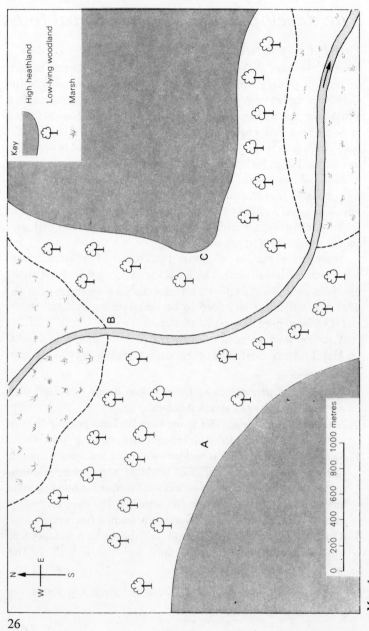

Map 1

To help you choose the best site, fill in Table 3.1 below. Give each site a mark out of 10 for each of the points 1–5. If a site does well on a point, give it high marks: if it does badly, give it low marks. (For example, site B will get higher marks for 'Nearness to the river. than site C.) The site with the highest total marks will be the best.

Table 3.1

Site	Point 1	Point 2	Point 3	Point 4	Point 5	Total
A						
B						
C						

The best site for the settlement is . . . .

Now you have decided which site is best for your settlement, draw in a stockade at the site on Map 1. The stockade will be the same size as the circle in Fig. 3.1 below. Within the stockade, you can draw in your own large hut and smaller ones for your followers (see Fig. 3.1).

Fig. 3.1

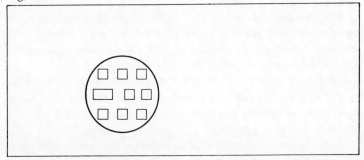

The next problem is to clear an area for farming, so that you can use your light ploughs. You can clear land up to 1000 metres round the settlement. It is not sensible to clear further than this, because there may be a sudden attack and all those who are farming will have to run back inside the stockade.

Draw a circle with a radius of 1000 metres (as shown on the scale to Map 1), with the stockade at its centre. The circle should be *lightly* drawn in pencil. This circle will roughly show the edge of the land for farming; but not all the land within the circle is useful. *The field can only be made on heathland.* Do *not* include the following in the field, even if they are within the circle:

(a) Marshes, which cannot be drained for farming.
(b) Woodland, which is very difficult to clear.
(c) Land on the other side of the river, which is hard to cross.

Now draw in the boundary of the field and name it 'Field 1'.

Part 2 The settlement grows

For the next five hundred years the settlement survives, but it does not increase in size as this is a time of difficulty and continual warfare. Among other troubles, in A.D. 875 a Viking raiding party comes up the river and plunders the first settlement seen. This is the settlement at site B (which is completely destroyed). The other two sites are hidden from the river by trees.

If you built your stockade at site B, you will now have to *rebuild* it at one of the other two sites. Also you will have to work out where your new Field 1 is going to be.

Time passes, and by the year 1050 England has become much more settled and peaceful under King Edward the Confessor, who has now ruled for eight years. As a result, the number of people in the settlement is increasing. This has two results:

First, new houses are needed. The stockade is too crowded for new houses, so they will have to be built *outside* the stockade, but as near to it as possible (so the new families can get back into the stockade in times of danger).

Draw in *ten* new houses (the same size as the smaller huts inside the stockade) close to the stockade.

Second, new fields are needed to provide food for the extra people. The thane (head of the village) has called a meeting of villagers to decide where to make a new field. It is now possible to clear and farm *woodland* because a heavy plough (pulled by oxen)

28

THE DEVELOPMENT OF THE MEDIEVAL TOWN

has been introduced. There are three other points to consider:

(a) The boundary of the new field must be within the 1000 metre circle (a convenient distance to walk).

(b) It is very difficult to get across the river with ploughs and animals, so land on the other side of the river is not suitable for farming.

(c) The new field should be as big as possible, to provide a large amount of food.

The meeting discusses all these points. When you have decided where the boundary of the new field should be, draw it in on Map 1. Name this area 'Field 2'.

The new field is a great success, and ten years later the number of villagers has increased again. Many of the villagers have been discussing whether the area across the river could be cleared for farming. As you are a member of one of the most important families in the village, you attend the village meeting (known as a *moot*) to talk about the problem.

It would be a good thing for the village to have land over the river, but if this land is to be farmed efficiently, a *bridge* will be needed. The question is: where would be the best place to build a bridge? You will have to think about the following points:

(a) The bridge must be as near as possible to the present village.

(b) It must allow as much land as possible to be cleared on the other side of the river. (Marshes cannot be drained for farming.)

(c) The river is roughly the same width and depth in most places.

When you have decided on a site for the bridge, mark it in on Map 1 (as shown in Fig. 3.2). Also mark in a track leading from the village to the bridge.

Fig. 3.2

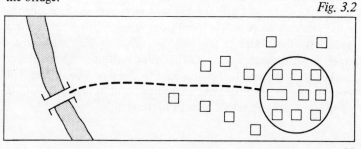

29

At the time the bridge is being built, the old village site (inside the stockade) has become very crowded. You and some of the other members of the moot decide to build new houses outside the stockade. You can put these houses where you like on Map 1 — but before you decide, consider the following:

(a)   It would be unwise to have your houses more than 600 metres from the stockade in case there is an attack on the area, either by men or wild animals (especially bears and packs of wolves).

(b)   It would be a good thing for the house to be near the river, which is a main source of water.

(c)   If your new house is near the bridge, it will be easy to reach the land which will be cleared on the other side of the river.

(d)   It is a good idea to have your house near the track, on which your cart can go.

When you have decided on a site for your new house, draw it in (the same size as the largest house inside the stockade) on Map 1. Then draw in about 10 or 15 similar houses in the same area. These are the new houses of other members of the moot, and also of new families which have been attracted to the area.

New farming land is now being cleared on the other side of the river. Land can be cleared up to 1000 metres from the bridge in any direction on that side of the river.

To help you to decide where the edge of the new field should be, draw in part of a circle with a radius of 1000 metres (see the scale) with its centre at the bridge. The new clearing should be as large as possible: it can include *heathland* and *woodland,* but *not* marshland, which is useless for farming. Name the new field 'Field 3'.

The population of England has now increased, as the country is more peaceful. More people travel from village to village to exchange goods. As the bridge is the only river-crossing in a wide area, a track grows on each side of it. This track continues the one already marked in, and extends from the east to the west side of Map 1. If possible, the track should run across heathland or fields, as there are robbers and dangerous wild animals in the uncleared woods.

Part 3 The Norman town

On Map 2, mark in the following: the edges of each field and the field names; the bridge; and the track (as in Map 1). Do *not* mark in the stockade as this has gradually been deserted by the villagers, who prefer new houses nearer the bridge. Draw in houses on each side of the track that runs from the site of the stockade to the bridge. Make each house slightly larger than it was before (something like Fig. 3.3).

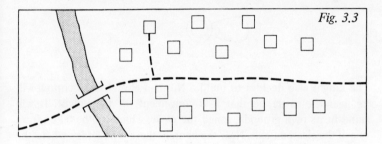

Fig. 3.3

After the Norman Conquest of 1066, William the Conqueror decides to grant all the area on Map 2 to one of his Norman knights. In return, the knight will fight for the King for up to forty days a year, or provide him with food when he needs it.

The Norman knight decides that the first thing he must do is to build a strong fort, in case the conquered Anglo-Saxon villagers rebel against him. The villagers have now been forced to become his serfs or slaves.

The knight therefore decides to build a 'motte and bailey' castle, because this is a simple form of defence which can be quickly constructed. The *motte* is a mound of earth with a small wooden fort on top. Next to the motte is the *bailey,* which is a flat area enclosed by a stockade. Both the motte and the bailey are surrounded by a deep ditch. Below is a plan of a motte and bailey castle from above, and section from the side:

Fig. 3.4

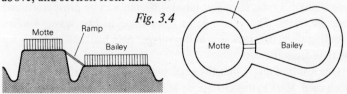

The castle must be close both to the village and to the track, so that the knight can control them. The knight can clear away villagers' houses if he wants in order to make room for his castle. Where would be the best place for the castle to go? When you have decided, draw in the motte and bailey castle on Map 2, making it the same size and shape as in Fig. 3.5.

Fig. 3.5

The knight also decides to build a Norman church. The church will be near the castle, so that it is convenient for the knight. It will stand in its own grounds, called the *glebe,* which will be taken from one of the cleared fields. Near the church there is a rectory where the priest lives. The church and rectory (within the glebe) are shown in plan in Fig. 3.6: the boundary of the glebe is the dotted line. Mark them in, the same size, on Map 2, making sure that the church is also reasonably convenient for the villagers who will want to worship there.

Fig. 3.6

King William I rules strongly: farming becomes more prosperous and trade increases. The village gains from trade in two ways. Traders travelling along the track stop at the village. Also boats bring goods up the river from the east.

One result of this is that the track becomes a rough road, as it is so much used. Mark in this change on Map 2: where the track runs, draw in a road (as shown in Fig. 3.7). Also, one of the larger houses becomes an inn to provide food and lodging for the travellers and traders. Mark this in also.

Fig. 3.7

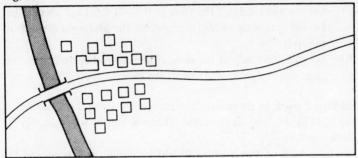

With the growth of trade, other changes take place:

(a) A *quay* (where ships are unloaded) is built along one bank of the river. It should be built near the bridge and will be about 100 metres long (see Fig. 8).

(b) Near the quay, merchants build *warehouses* for storing goods. These warehouses are larger than normal houses (see Fig. 3.8).

Fig. 3.8

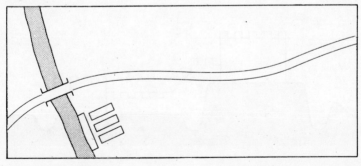

Look carefully at Map 2. Think where the quay and warehouses should be built. When you have decided, draw them in on the map, the same size as in Fig. 3.8.

33

Since the Conquest, England has prospered and many towns have grown rich through trade. Because of this, more people come to live in towns, and build themselves houses.

In this town, houses spread in two areas:

(a) On the same side of the river as the old stockade used to be. Houses spread up to 600 metres from the bridge on this side of the river.

(b) On the *other* side of the river. Houses spread up to 200 metres from the bridge on that side of the river.

On Map 2 mark in these new houses, making them the same size as the huts in the original stockade. The new houses will probably be close together.

The family of the Norman knight has continued to control the town. The Norman lord collects taxes from the merchants and towns-folk, and as the town grows richer he becomes very wealthy.

In 1135 a terrible civil war breaks out when King Stephen's claim to the throne is challenged by Queen Matilda. The grandson of the Norman knight has grown rich and become a baron, and so he decides to improve the defences of his motte and bailey castle. He therefore builds a stone tower on the motte and puts stone walls round the bailey (see Fig. 3.9).

Fig. 3.9

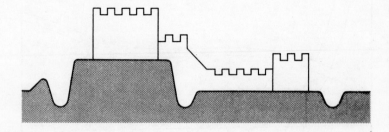

Draw in the new stone castle in the same place as the old motte and bailey castle. (Rub out the original pencil marks if necessary.) The
34

new castle has a large stone tower on the motte, and two small stone towers at the corners of the bailey (as in Fig. 3.10).

Fig. 3.10

During the civil war, many towns have been attacked and plundered. They have therefore appealed to King Stephen to grant them *charters*. If the King allows them to buy a charter from him, the town will be able to:

(a) build defensive walls to keep raiding soldiers out;
(b) govern itself through its own aldermen (chief citizens);
(c) control its own trade (which the local baron controls at present);
(d) stop paying feudal dues. This is money or goods that the towns-folk pay to the baron, who is meant to hand it on to the King twice a year.

The problem for King Stephen is: will he gain by granting charters to towns? There are a number of arguments for and against the idea, so the King calls a Great Council of barons to ask for advice. As a baron, you are invited to attend this Great Council. It is important that you should think carefully what is *best for the King:* if King Stephen suspects that you are only thinking of yourself as a baron, and giving him poor advice, he may take your castle and all your lands away from you.

From the point of view of the King, the reasons *for* selling charters are:

1. The King would get a large amount of money, as towns are prepared to pay well for a charter. With this money, the King could hire troops (mercenaries) to help win the civil war.

2. The town will be able to build walls and defend itself. So the King will no longer have to come to its defence if it is attacked by the enemy.
3. The feudal dues which the town pays to the baron sometimes fail to reach the King. Either the baron keeps the money, or it is impossible to collect it because of the war. A single large sum would be better.

According to how important each of these points is for the King, give it a mark out of 10. If you think the point is very important, give it 8 or 9 out of 10. If it seems unimportant, give it 2 or 3 out of 10. Write the marks in Table 3.2 below.

Table 3.2

Point	Marks out of 10
1	
2	
3	
Total	

The reasons *against* selling charters are:

4. The town may desert to the enemy when it gets its charter and becomes independent.
5. Once the charter is sold, the King will never again be able to raise feudal dues from it twice a year. The charter cannot be taken back by the King once it is sold.
6. If the town builds walls, it will be extremely difficult to besiege it successfully if it turns against the King.

According to how important you think each of these arguments is for the King, give it a mark out of 10 (as for Table 3.2). Write the marks
36

in Table 3.3 below

Table 3.3

Point	Marks out of 10
4	
5	
6	
Total	

If the total for Table 3.2 is the larger, the advice is *for* granting charters: if the total for Table 3.3 is larger, the advice is *against* granting charters.

My advice to King Stephen is *grant/do not grant* charters.

Part 4 The medieval town

King Stephen received a good deal of advice from his Great Council of barons, but not all the barons advised the same thing. When the town on Map 2 appealed for a charter, the King decided to play safe:

(a) He refused to allow the town to build walls, in case it turned against him.

(b) He allowed the town to govern itself, control its own trade and stop paying feudal dues. In return, the town paid him a large sum of money.

The town, in fact, was granted a *liberty* — a list of privileges. Aldermen were elected, and now that the town controlled its own trade, each craft (e.g. weavers, shoemakers) formed a *guild*.

The *craft guild* controlled *every* aspect of the craft. For instance, the Shoemakers' Guild allowed *only* its members to make or sell shoes in the town. No one else was permitted to do this. The guild fixed the price of shoes, and laid down hours of work for shoemakers.

37

It fined members who made poor quality shoes. Three times a year, the guild arranged a huge feast for all its members.

You would be allowed to join a guild in your teens. You would first become an *apprentice,* and work for seven years learning the craft. Apprentices received almost no money. They were a wild lot and often had riots. If you learnt your trade well, you would next become a *journeyman* for seven years. You could now earn a little money, as you would be paid by the day (*journée* in French). At the end of that time, the head of the guild would send for you. He would ask to see your most perfect piece of work — your masterpiece. If this was good enough, you could become a *master* of the guild.

The guilds became more and more prosperous. After the civil war, there was about forty years of peace in England, and trade increased.

It is now 1189, and King Richard I has just come to the throne. He has immediately decided to go on a crusade to recapture Jerusalem, which has been taken by the Turks. The King needs to raise a large sum of money quickly to pay for knights, stores and ships — so he is willing to sell charters to towns. Is this the moment for the town to try to buy a charter which will allow the town to build walls?

What is your opinion? Consider the following points about building walls and gates:

1. The town would be safer from outside attack.
2. Defences would encourage trade, as merchants would know that their goods would be safe in a walled town.
3. It would stop people smuggling goods into the town against the rules of the guilds.
4. It would add to the pride of the town.
5. Criminals inside the town would find it harder to commit crimes and get away from it. A robber could not escape out of a walled town once the alarm was given: he would be stopped by the guards on the town gates.
6. A charter will cost a lot of money. All the guilds and everyone who owns a house will have to pay.
7. If any houses are in the way of where the walls are going to be built, these houses will be knocked down.
8. If walls are built the town can resist attack. But if attackers do

38

eventually get in, they will be so furious that they may kill everybody in sight. At present, attackers just take what plunder they can, and then go away.

9. The walls may not enclose the whole town. Some of the poorer houses on the edge of the town may be left outside.

10. The walls will have to be manned by soldiers. This will mean that the townsfolk will either have to do guard duty themselves, or have to hire soldiers to do it.

There are great arguments in the town about these points. On Whit Sunday when there are feasts throughout the town, the townsfolk have gathered around the market cross in the middle of the town. Some of the people there are mentioned in the *Information sheet* below. Do you think the majority of the townsfolk present would have been in favour of building walls, or against it?

The majority of townsfolk present would have been *for/against* buying a charter and building walls.

Information sheet

The baron He has come to the town for the feasting. The town's walls would link up with his stone castle and make it stronger. However, a walled town *might* decide to stop him entering it. At present he can come into the town with a band of soldiers when he likes.

Master of the Tanners' Guild He is drunk — as usual: it helps to take his mind off the terrible smell of the tanning process. He has gathered that the charter and wall-building will cost him and his guild money.

Journeyman of the Carpenters' Guild He has just got married, so he wants to be sure that his house will be safe. But he can scarcely afford to pay a penny in extra taxes.

Master of the Goldsmiths' Guild He is by far the richest man in town and so he is mainly worried about keeping his money and treasure safe.

Apprentice of the Clothworkers' Guild He is always stealing scraps of cloth to give to a girl in a nearby village. If the town had walls, the gates would be shut at dusk — so he would find it very difficult to go on seeing his girl in the evenings.

Apprentice of the Fishmongers' Guild When there are no boats unloading fish (from the coast) at the quay, he can get away from his master and play football. This is very dangerous. It is played through the streets: there are no rules and players often get clubbed or knifed, and sometimes killed. Town gates would make good goals; but the walls might mean that the town could be controlled more easily and there would be fewer riotous games.

Journeyman of the Goldsmiths' Guild He is finding it hard to get work, because few of the townsfolk want gold ornaments or jewellery. They bury any gold they have, to keep it safe.

A crippled soldier As a young man, he fought for the baron during the civil war. He was wounded and lost both his legs. He is now old and poor, but he still lives in his own little cottage by the river. He is afraid that the cottage might be knocked down to make way for the walls.

A beggar During the day he seems to be completely crippled; but every night he regains the use of his legs and secretly goes out stealing. If the town had gates, he could sit by them during the day: many travellers would pass him, and he might beg a good sum of money. On the other hand, he might get caught stealing: he could no longer escape out of a walled town.

Inn-keeper If the town had walls, more travellers would spend the night at his inn, as they would feel safe even if the town was attacked.

Apprentice of the Tanners' Guild Life is very dull, working six days a week for the drunken master tanner. The only bright spots are fights with apprentices of other guilds, and games such as football. If the town had walls, these might be stopped.

Master of the Armourers' Guild One of the main things he makes are weapons (swords, spears, arrowheads etc.) At present, every man in the town is armed: if there were walls, many of the townsfolk might feel so safe that they would not bother to buy swords. On the other hand, the walls would need guards, and guards need weapons. Only the Armourers' Guild members can sell weapons in the town.

Night-watchman He walks round the town during the night, shouting out the time each hour. He is meant to catch thieves, but this is
40

almost impossible at present: if the thieves are seen and chased, they run out of the town and escape into the woods.

An old man He still farms a few strips outside the town. If there were walls and gates, he would have further to walk to his strips. He has lived in the town all his life, and the town has survived without walls. Why build them now?

The priest What worries him is whether the church and rectory will be *inside* the new walls or *outside*. If they are outside, it will be worse than if there were no walls: a band of robbers, finding it impossible to get into the town, would destroy everything outside it. If the church and rectory were inside the walls, they would be safe.

Alderman He is a very old man, but he can still vividly remember the day during the civil war when a band of soldiers attacked the town, and carried off all his possessions and his young and beautiful wife. He feels that no cost is too great to stop that sort of thing happening.

A runaway serf He has just escaped from a nearby village, where he worked on the land of a harsh lord. If he can stay in the town for a year and a day, he will become a free man (at present, he is almost a slave). But the lord may come at any time with a band of soldiers (retainers) to look for him. As there are no walls round the town, it would be hard to stop the lord doing this at present.

Journeyman of the Masons' Guild If walls are built, this will mean work and money for him. However, the aldermen may invite one of the bands of travelling ('free') masons to do all the work for the new walls: in this case the journeyman will get no benefit.

Part 5 The town defences
Many townsfolk were against the idea of applying for a charter to build walls round the town; but it was the aldermen who had the final say in the matter. The aldermen are mostly rich and old: they were mainly concerned with *safety*. They therefore decided to ask the King for a charter.

King Richard wishes to raise money quickly for the Third Crusade: he willingly sold the charter to the town.

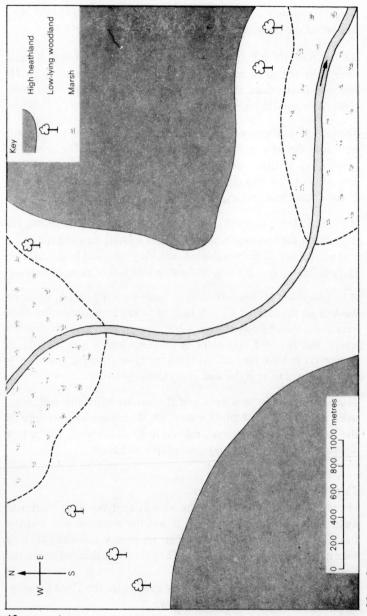

Key

High heathland

Low-lying woodland

Marsh

N
W E
S

0   200   400   600   800   1000 metres

Map 2

The problem for the town now is: where should be walls be built? Consider the following points:

1. It would be a good thing for the town walls to join up with the Baron's castle. This would make the defences stronger.
2. There is only enough money to build *ten* separate towers, joined by walls. Two towers close together can form a gateway. (Towers and walls should be drawn in as is shown in Fig. 3.11.)
3. The walling should be straight, if possible. This makes walls quicker and cheaper to build.
4. There must not be more than 400 metres of wall without a tower, or else the walls will be very difficult to defend.
5. It would be wise to put walling along the river, in case attackers come by ship. This may mean that it is not possible to wall *both* halves of the town.
6. There should not be more walling than is absolutely necessary: this would only lead to extra expense and be harder to defend.

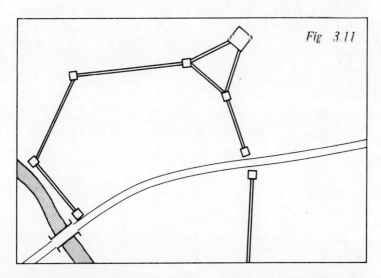

Fig 3.11

Mark in on Map 2 where you think the town should build its walls and towers.

Now compare Map 1 with Map 2 to see some of the stages in the the development of a town.

References

Blair, PH. *Roman Britain and Early England.* 55 B.C.–A.D. 871, Nelson, 1963.

Blair, PH. *An Introduction to Anglo-Saxon England,* Cambridge University Press, 1956.

Brooke, CNL. *The Saxon and Norman Kings,* Batsford, 1963.

Brooke, CNL. *From Alfred to Henry III, 871-1272,* Nelson, 1961.

Coulton, GG. *Social Life in Britain from the Conquest to the Reformation,* Cambridge University Press, 1919.

Davis, RHC. *King Stephen: 1135-1154,* Longmans, 1967.

Douglas, DC. *William the Conqueror,* Eyre & Spottiswoode, 1964.

Haskins, CH. *The Renaissance of the Twelfth Century,* Harvard University Press, 1927.

Pirenne, H. *Medieval Cities,* Princeton University Press. 1925.

Vinogradov, PG. *Society in the Eleventh Century,* Oxford University Press, 1908.

Whitelocke, D (ed). *The Norman Conquest: its setting and impact,* Eyre & Spottiswoode, 1966.

4

Frontier

Frontier is a group role-play designed for the nine to fifteen years age range. It aims to place the pupils in the position of early colonists of British North America, and to show some of the problems and opportunities which faced them at various stages of colonial development from about 1690 to 1783. Also, it intends to demonstrate the concept of the Frontier in American history. The *Information sheet* (p. 61) and the *Colonial characters* (p. 58) are based on historical fact.

The simulation is designed for class or group use. Up to five pupils can form a group to play each game of *Frontier*. The game can last up to four 40-minute periods.

Framework

The game	*Historical actuality*
The pupils represent different types of early colonists who intend to settle in the colonial areas 1-5 of British North America (Map 4). They can settle the regions shown on the map.	There was a wide range of early British settlers, from fur trappers and traders to tobacco merchants and plantation owners.

The map shows the five main colonial areas for settlement in the 1690s. The squares indicate the regions which the players can settle. From a point on the East Coast, the players settle squares in their colonial areas.

The five regions on the map cover the areas of New England (colony 1), the Middle Colonies (colonies 2 and 3) and the Southern Colonies (colonies 4 and 5). The points on the East Coast are: 1. Boston; 2. New York; 3. Washington; 4. Charlestown; 5. Brunswick.

A letter in a square indicates the possibility of growing a certain crop or exploiting raw materials. Additional revenues are drawn from these squares.

By the 1690s, the colonies were already developing their own distinctive characters, influenced by the type of economies they were able to develop. Crops and raw materials ranged from wheat, fur and timber to sugar, rice and indigo.

The players have to observe the colonial boundaries, the international frontiers, and the Indian Line. The Indian Line indicates a change in the nature of settlement to the west of it.

Each colony operated within its own frontiers. The international boundary to the north and west is that fixed by the 1783 Treaty of Paris, while the southern boundary is that of Spanish Florida. The Indian Line represents the Proclamation Line of 1763 which ran along the Appalachian mountains. It was laid down by the British government to prevent the further westward expansion of the colonies after Pontiac's rebellion.

The rules warn the players of the possible penalties if they settle squares on or to the west of the Indian Line.

Lord Dunmore's war of 1774 between Kentucky settlers who were to the west of the Proclamation Line, and Indians, showed the danger of uncontrolled westwards expansion.

Each player takes the role of a colonial character, and has to choose a suitable colonial area for settlement. Each colonial area is different.

From the point they choose, the players settle up to three squares a round. They follow the procedure laid down in the rules. The players first settle all squares within their own colonial area's boundaries, and then Indian Line squares, and squares to the west.

The players receive revenue from the squares they have settled. Different amounts of revenue are gained from different types of square.

In the notes on *Colonial characters* accurate historical information is given about different types of early colonists. Early settlers chose the regions most suitable to them — for example, in the early eighteenth century some 250,000 Germans from the Palatinate settled in Pennsylvania and Virginia as religious refugees. The *Information sheet* shows the state of the colonies in the 1690s.

Population pressure, both from immigration and natural expansion, resulted in the steady westward expansion of settlements within the colonial boundaries. In 1749 the Ohio Company was founded for the settlement of the upper Ohio river and trading within that region. In 1768 pressure from the American colonists forced the British government to extend the Proclamation Line to the west.

By the mid-eighteenth century the colonial economies had become highly developed. In New England small-scale farming was widespread, and shipbuilding, forestry, iron-making and distilling molasses were firmly established. In the Middle Colonies farms were on a larger scale, and New York and Pennsylvania were at the heart of the 'bread colonies'. Trade and industry flourished, with the rapid expansion of the triangular trades between Britain— North and South America—the West

47

Indies and Africa. In the Southern Colonies a plantation economy emerged, particularly with the increase in the import of slaves after 1697. Tobacco, rice and indigo were exported in return for manufactured goods.

The Chance sheet mirrors factors which influenced much of early colonial settlement. Among the questions dealt with are the establishment of trade and commerce, the danger of Indian wars, the question of French intervention in alliance with the Indians, the fluctuating fortunes in the production and sale of colonial commodities, the danger of natural disasters, and the outbreaks of hostility between the colonists and the British government.

By the eighteenth century the New England colonies were prospering from the exploitation of the Newfoundland Fisheries. Indian wars were a permanent problem, such as the Yemassee War from 1715 to 1718 which threatened the existence of Carolina. The intervention of the French on the side of the Indians was a major concern. The defeat of General Braddock in 1755 by the French and the Indians threatened the British position in North America. The enforcement of the Navigation Acts could threaten the colonial economies. Also, in 1732-33 the extension of the excise to tobacco was narrowly averted. The problem of disease on the plantations was serious, and a feature of advertisements for slaves was that they had already had smallpox, and were therefore immune. The Boston Port Act of 1774 closed Boston in retaliation for the Boston Tea Party.

Equipment

Apart from the text, two dice per game (or scissors and used matchsticks for the spinners) and pencils and erasers.

Playing procedure

1. If a class activity, the class is divided into groups of up to five players. The game should not be played by fewer than four players. If four players, settle areas 1–4 on the map.
2. Cut out the spinners or use two dice. One pair of spinners or dice is sufficient for each group of players.
3. Read through the text with the class, explaining problems as they arise. The choice of trading areas can take the form of a class activity.
4. Choice of colonial areas as a class activity:

   (a) It is recommended that the notes on *Colonial characters* are read aloud, with different pupils taking different characters' parts.
   (b) Within each group of players, allocate each pupil a different character's role. Try to ensure that each character has about the same number of pupils identifying with him.
   (c) Read the *Information sheet* for each colonial area, preferably aloud, and allow the pupils to fill in Table 4.1 for each of the three factors, with them bearing in mind the role of the characters they have taken.
   (d) When the tables have been filled in, the decisions of the different characters can be announced to the class, with the pupils, if required, explaining the reasons for their decisions. They can try to get other players to agree with their choice, or change their previous decisions, if already announced. When all the characters have made their final choices, these can be recorded in a table on the blackboard.
   (e) The colony with the largest number of pupils deciding to settle in it can be declared the one most likely to expand. Those who have chosen it can be told to place 5 in the balance column for Round 1.

5. Choice of colonial area as a group activity. Pupils within each group of players can be allocated a different role, or be allowed to choose one from within the list of characters, following the read-

Map 4

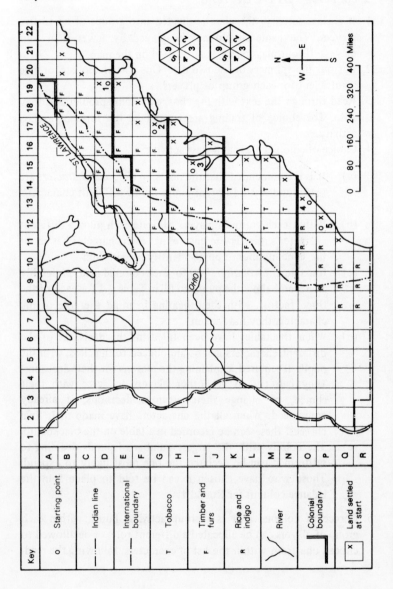

ing out of the notes of *Colonial characters*. They can then fill in Table 4.1.

Or

If desired, the notes on *Colonial characters* need not be consulted, and the pupils can judge the colonial areas on the basis of the *Information sheet*. When they fill in Table 4.1, they will have to be told to ignore the *Colonial characters* notes.

6. Work through settlement and revenue procedures. Players can colour in boundaries etc. on the map to make them clearer, and acquaint them with the key before play begins.

7. In settling it helps if each pupil, at his turn, carefully numbers the square he settles with his own number; and on other players' turns numbers, with *their* number, the squares which *they* settle. In this way a picture will emerge of the westward expansion of all the colonies, and confusion over the settlement of certain squares will be avoided.

8. Players can keep a journal of the progress of their settlement. In this they will state the amount of territory they have settled, the impact of chance factors, the amount of revenues they have gained and the fortunes of the other colonies.

Frontier

Map 4 shows the outline of North America during the early period of British settlement from about 1690 to 1783. Each square on the map represents an area a group of colonists have settled or can settle. Squares which have already been settled are indicated on the map (see key). Points 1–5 are areas from which the colonies can continue to expand. It is expected that each colony will have been able to expand up to the Indian Line on the map by the 1780s.

You represent a group of colonists who will try to colonize the area on the map from one of the points 1–5 marked on the East Coast.

Previous settlers and explorers have given you the following information about the whole area:

1. Blank squares are suitable for the growing of grain and the rearing of cattle. Squares already settled are of this nature.

2. Squares marked F can supply furs and timber.

51

3. Squares marked R can be used for growing rice and indigo (a dye).
4. Squares marked T can be used for growing tobacco.
5. *Squares through which the Indian Line runs can only be settled at the risk of provoking an Indian War.* The same applies to all squares to the *west* of the Indian Line, where there is also a danger from the French. Chance Sheet no. 2 shows what may happen if you settle in such squares.

As a colonist your aim will be to make your colony the richest. To do so, follow the rules below. *Read the rules through carefully before you begin, otherwise you will be at a disadvantage.*

Rules

1. Read through the notes on *Colonial characters* carefully. As one of the characters, you have to choose one of the points 1–5 on the East Coast (see Map) from which to expand your colony. To help you decide which point, consider the following factors:

Factors

(a) Conditions for the pursuit of the character's most important interest, whether religious, commercial, agricultural etc.

(b) The number of squares which can be settled from that point, up to and including the Indian Line squares, and the possibilities for further expansion to the West.

(c) The number of resource squares within the colony, marked F, T or R – with particular reference to the character's commercial interests.

2. Read through the *Information sheet,* and for each of the factors above, give each colonial area (1–5) marks out of five according to the following scale:

Very favourable	5 marks
Favourable	4
Quite favourable	3
Not very favourable	2
Unfavourable	1-0

When you have marked each colonial area for the factors, place the marks for each in Table 4.1.

Table 4.1

Factor	Colony 1	Colony 2	Colony 3	Colony 4	Colony 5
a					
b					
c					
Total					

Colonize the colonial area with the highest mark. If you have chosen the same colonial area as another player in your group, throw a dice or use a spinner to decide who colonizes that area. (If there is a draw, throw again.) If you cannot settle your first choice, try and settle your second choice. If another player has that area higher on his list of choices he has priority. In that case, try your third choice, and so on.

3. Order of play. The player who has colonial area 1 has the first turn, the player with area 2, the second turn, etc.
4. Before his turn each player throws the dice or uses the spinners to see which number on the *Chance sheet* he has. Follow the instructions opposite that number.
5. Each player can settle up to *three squares* each round, unless a *Chance card* says otherwise.

Settling
(a) In Round 1 settling starts from the numbered square the player has chosen. This square counts as an already settled square.
(b) A player can settle a square which shares a border with a square already settled. A border is one edge of a square.

Fig. 4.1

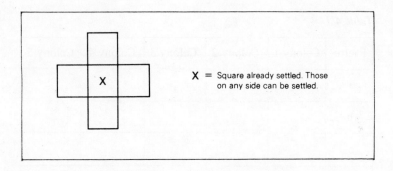

X = Square already settled. Those on any side can be settled.

(c) Only squares can be settled. This includes squares which extend over the sea or the international boundary line (see key on map).

(d) Players can only settle within their *own* colonial area's squares, including Indian Line squares. They cannot cross the colony boundaries.

(e) Before expanding into areas to the west of the Indian Line players must have settled all squares in their colonies up to and including Indian Line squares.

(f) If a player is boxed in by another player or players, and cannot settle any more squares, he can then go and settle the square which is nearest the last square he settled. From that square he can continue to expand as before.

(g) Number in any square settled on the map. Once this is done a player cannot change his decision. Each player numbers in on his map the squares which other players have settled.

(h) For each round the player can keep a diary of the progress of his settlement.

6. *Revenues*

Once a square has been settled, it will yield revenues for that round, and for *all future rounds*. At the end of his turn a player gains the following revenues from his settled squares, including those which were settled when he started colonizing.

Table 4.2

Type of square	Marked	Units of revenue per turn
Rice and indigo	R	2
Tobacco	T	2
Timber and fur	F	2
Grain and cattle	Blank	1

A player should follow any instructions (on the *Chance sheet)* relating to revenues he received that turn. Then place the revenues for that turn in the Revenues column of the Balance sheet. Add together the revenues and the Balance for that round. Place the total in the Balance column for the next round.

Each square settled will yield revenues for that turn and for every following turn of the player. See example below.

Fig. 4.2

Round	Balance	Revenues
3	15	6
4	21	14
5	35	

Fig. 4.2. shows the addition of scores for each round.

At the start of Round 3 the Balance was 15. The revenues for that turn were 6, so the new Balance for Round 4 was 21. In Round 4 the revenues were 14, thus for Round 5 the balance is 35.

7. A round is completed when each player has had his turn.
8. The game ends when all squares are settled, or after an agreed number of rounds.
9. The player with the highest total in the Balance column at the end of the game will be the winner.

Balance sheet

Round	Balance	Revenues
1	0	
2		
3		
4		
5		
6		
7		
8		
9		
10		
11		
12		
13		
14		
15		

Chance sheet

Chance number

1. The player who has settled colonial area 1 receives a bonus of 10 units, which represents the profits made by the colony's trade in fish, timber and rum to the West Indies.

2. An Indian war has broken out, with the Indians receiving the open backing of the French. The French supply them with muskets. If you have settled an Indian Line square, or a square to the west of the Indian Line, your colony will be at war with the Indians. Large areas will be devastated, and you will need all your balance and revenues for resettlement. There will be no colonial expansion for this round, and you will also *place nought* (0) *in the balance column for the next round.*

3. A hurricane has caused widespread damage, and the colony cannot expand for this turn.

4. Tobacco smoking has increased in popularity in England. The price for tobacco has greatly risen. For any tobacco square which has already been *settled*, double the income for that round.

5. The government has imposed excise (a tax) on tobacco. The increase in price has caused a fall in the sale of tobacco. For that round receive *one* unit only of revenue for each tobacco square settled.

6. War has broken out between England and France. Trade between the colony and England has declined, with ships being attacked by French privateers (ships with a licence to be pirates). The French have also attacked the colony from the west, with Indian support. You receive no revenues for that turn, and you also take 20 units from the balance.

7. Religious persecution in Europe has greatly increased the number of settlers arriving. The colony can expand up to 5 squares for that round.

8. War with France has ended. There has been a sharp fall in the demand for timber from the colony. The revenues from squares marked F drop to *one* unit of revenue per square for that turn.

9. A dispute with the British government over illegal trade has led to the closing of the colony's main port. For this turn, receive no revenues.

10. The increase in the output of sugar from the sugar colonies of the West Indies has meant a sharp increase in the demand for rice from North America to feed the slaves. The price of rice has therefore greatly increased. For this turn, *double* the revenues for 'Rice and Indigo' squares, marked R, already settled.

11. The War with France has greatly increased the demand for timber for the British navy. Revenues are therefore doubled from 'Timber and Fur' squares, marked F, for this turn.

12. Fever has broken out among the slaves on the rice plantations. Many of them have been wiped out, which greatly cuts the revenue from rice plantations. For this turn, receive only *one* unit of revenue from each rice square settled, marked R.

Colonial characters

1. Fur Trapper

Ever since the decrease in the Russian fur trade from about 1600 there has been a growing demand for furs from North America. The explorations of a Frenchman, La Salle, revealed the fortunes to be made from fur trapping stations. The fur trapper is interested in founding such centres in the interior. From these he can exchange axes, beads, muskets, mirrors etc. for furs which the Indians will bring to him. In time he will be able to employ his own men as fur trappers. The fur station will be fortified to protect it from hostile Indian attacks, and from the French, who will be his rivals. The best site for such a centre would be in the valley of a major river with its mouth on the east coast of North America.

2. Fur Trader

He is the youngest son of a Bristol merchant who has just died after making a fortune from trading in slaves to the West Indies and from commerce between North America and England. The son has been left a small furtune with which to establish his own business. For a time he was his father's agent in North America, and he has decided to establish his own business, concentrating on the fur trade. Furs are in demand, especially for hats and winter coats. In this business he will employ trappers, such as character 1. The best place to base his firm will be a region with maximum opportunities for fur trapping.

3. Protestant Rebel

He is the leader of a group of protestants who have fallen out with the the rulers of the colony. As the rebels' leader he has refused to accept the religious demands of the majority of the colonists, which include an oath of loyalty. The rebels are not allowed to vote in the elections for the colonial assembly. The leader of the rebels therefore intends to lead his followers into a new region, driving their cattle before them and carrying their goods in covered waggons. The group is formed mainly of small grain farmers.

4. Huguenot Immigrant

This man is an old, cautious figure. He has been chosen as the representative of a group of Huguenot refugees, who were driven out of France in 1685 by the King of France, Louis XIV. The Huguenots were skilled cloth weavers, and he is therefore very interested in the weaving centres which have sprung up along the coastline for the weaving of wool. The Huguenots are mainly interested in following their trade free from religious persecution. As such, their leader has heard of William Penn, and the Huguenots appear willing to go and settle in Penn's colonial area. Money is no problem, as the Huguenots are quite wealthy.

5. Northern Merchant

His brother has died, and left him a trading vessel. He is very interested in the prosperous and expanding trade with the West Indies. The main exports there are flour, fish, meat and timber, in return for sugar and molasses. The sugar and molasses are used for distilling into rum, and he intends to build a distillery in the interior if his trade prospers. He is very interested in colonial expansion, as this will mean new settlers who will increase both the output of flour and cattle for export, and consume imports. Also, the settlers will provide workers for the distillery.

6. *Shipbuilder*

Following the accession in 1685 of James II (who is widely suspected of helping Catholics and likely to persecute Puritans) this Puritan has decided to flee to North America and set himself up in business as a shipbuilder. He is very interested in basing himself on an area with a good supply of timber. In time he expects to be able to expand his business, and provide ships for the trade between North America, England and the West Indies, and between the different North American colonies. He would also expect to provide naval supplies for the English government.

7. *Land Speculator*

A shady character, he is a friend of the king, and has considerable influence at court. The king owes him money, and as repayment for this debt the speculator has pressed the king to give him a grant of land in one of the North American colonies. Particularly he is interested in land which can be sold to other speculators or plantation owners interested in the commercial crops of tobacco, rice and indigo. To spur him on he has the examples of Lord Baltimore, who in 1632 received the grant of Maryland from Charles I, and of the noblemen who in 1664 were given a grant of New Jersey by Charles II.

8. *Merchant*

He is a friend of the land speculator, and is willing to invest a fortune in the opening up of rice and tobacco plantations in the Southern Colonies. With the development of the slave trade between Africa and the North American colonies a plentiful supply of labour is available. From what his agents in North America tell him, there is the possibility of selling large quantities of rice to the West Indian plantations. The increasing demand for tobacco makes this an attractive investment area as well.

9. *Tobacco Merchant*

In 1587 Sir Walter Raleigh received some tobacco from his Virginia Colony, and introduced the habit to the court of Queen Elizabeth. In 1613 tobacco was first successfully cured in large enough quantities for it to be shipped commercially to England. By the 1630s over 60

150,000 pounds of tobacco a year were being imported into England. The attempts of the government to stamp out tobacco smoking ended in the 1650s. The tobacco merchant is the son of an early tobacco-seller in London. He has decided to set himself up as an agent for the tobacco trade in America, and will base himself on one of the southern ports. He will be willing to lend the tobacco planters the money they need to expand their plantations.

10. Tobacco Planter

He knows the tobacco merchant, character 9. He himself came out to America as a poor man who had signed on as a labourer. Through hard work he made a small fortune from trading in cloth, and he has sold his business to a Huguenot. With this money he has decided to buy some land in the South and clear it for a tobacco plantation. If he is successful, he has plans to expand his tobacco plantations: he is married and has ten children, six of them sons, who will want to to run their own plantations when they grow up. He is looking forward to plantation life; he intends to build a large country mansion. This he will fill with expensive furniture, glass, china and pictures from England. The growing of tobacco is very easy, and he knows how to handle labourers and slaves.

Information sheet

By the 1690s the British had founded a number of colonies on the east coast of North America. To the early British settlers America had appeared as the promised land, being a haven of freedom and potentially prosperous. In South America the Spanish had shown the way, destroying the Aztec and Inca civilizations and gaining vast amounts of gold and silver. In their quest for treasure, English adventurers had mounted mainly buccaneering expeditions, although there had been attempts at settlement. Most of these had been ill-fated: by 1588 Sir Walter Raleigh's expeditions to Virginia had ended in disaster. Also, an earlier discovery of 'gold' proved to be mistaken. The ore which Martin Frobisher's ships returned with was finally used as rubble to cover the roads of Deptford. By the early seventeenth century more realistic reasons were emerging for establishing British colonies in North America.

Some settlers, such as the Pilgrim Fathers, wished to escape from religious persecution. The majority of religious refugees were Puritans, escaping from persecution in England and on the Continent. Other settlers founded colonies, such as Virginia, in order to make money. Commercial interests hoped to get fortunes from the sale of land, the growing of commercial crops such as sugar cane and indigo, and a developing shipping industry. The early British settlements were bustling, expanding communities which were already noted for their independent and aggressive attitudes. However, they were hemmed in by the French and Indians to the north and the west, and the Spanish to the south.

New England: Region 1

This region covers the four nothernmost colonies. It is formed from New Hampshire, Massachusetts, Rhode Island and Connecticut. Forests are widespread, the soil is poor and the climate harsh. Life is difficult for the settlers. Many of them belong to different Puritan sects, and the first settlers here were those who arrived on the Mayflower in 1620. They founded New Plymouth and did well, after early hardships. In 1630 the Massachusetts Bay Company was formed by a group of protestants. This led to the establishment of the port of Boston and a flourishing colony. The trickle of colonists then became a flood, so that by the 1690s there are a number of colonies in the area. These are often based on protestant communities which after bitter quarrels broke away from existing settlements. The colonies rely on farming, shipbuilding, fishing and trade. Already there is a major trade in timber and fish which are sent to the West Indies in exchange for molasses to make rum.

The colonies have their own elected assemblies and trouble has already arisen between them and the British government over the control of trade. Massachusetts refused to obey the Navigation Acts, which forbade the Massachusetts' merchants from trading directly to Europe. Therefore in 1684 the colony lost its charter, and later it was placed directly under royal rule. In 1689, after the Glorious Revolution had placed William III on the throne, the new king returned the colonies their rights.

The Middle Colonies: Regions 2 and 3

The colonies of New York, New Jersey and Pennsylvania form this region. The area is a melting pot for different races and religions. The main non-British element are the Dutch. In 1664, the Dutch colony of New Netherlands surrendered to the British, who changed its name to New York. Other races include Swedes, Germans, Scots, Irish and French protestant refugees (the Huguenots). In 1681 William Penn, a Quaker, was given permission to found the colony of Pennsylvania; this was in settlement of a debt owed him by the King, Charles II. Pennsylvania has served as a centre for Quaker immigrants. As William Penn believes in selling land cheaply or letting it for low rents, Pennsylvania attracts large numbers of colonists.

New York is a great commercial centre. It has contacts with the interior, and has established a flourishing fur trade along the Hudson valley, much to the annoyance of the French. A growing number of masts can be seen along the New York waterfront, since grain and meat are exported along with furs. Imports range from French wines to African slaves.

All three colonies have had their own elected assemblies since 1689 and they largely control their own internal affairs. Each colony has a governor appointed by the king of England.

Southern Colonies: Regions 4 and 5

Since the foundation of Jamestown in 1607 as the first settlement of the Virginia Company, a planters' society has developed in the Southern Colonies. Region 4 is made up of large estates owned by a handful of established families. The main crop is tobacco, and it is so important that colonial officials and clergymen receive it as their wages. The tobacco is exported direct to England, where tobacco smoking is fashionable. In return, there are imported from England luxury items, which the planters require to furnish their new and magnificent mansions. In region 5 the main crop is no longer tobacco. The area has a warm, moist climate, and with its low-lying land it is suitable for growing rice, indigo and sugar cane.

The planters in both areas rely upon Negro slave labour, the 'black ivory' imported from Africa. Slaves are sold in the markets at auctions, and once bought they have to sweat and toil in slave gangs on the plantations. The planters also use criminals transported from

England and workers who have 'signed on' for a number of years. The plantations are profitable, so the planters are eager to expand their estates into new areas. Also, the soil of their estates becomes poor very quickly through the growing of tobacco and sugar.

These colonies have different forms of government. In 1624 Virginia became a royal colony under direct royal rule after being privately run by the Virginia Company. Virginia has its own assembly, and a tradition of control over its own internal affairs. To the north of Virginia is Maryland, which from 1632 until 1688 was the private property of the Baltimore family. Maryland served as a centre for Catholic refugees. To the South is Carolina, a colony originally in the hands of courtiers of Charles II. Carolina has not flourished, despite being founded solely as a commercial concern.

French Territory to the North and West, Spanish Territory to the South

The region to the north of the International Boundary is firmly under the control of the French. After the pioneering explorations of Samuel de Champlain, founder of Quebec in 1608, the French have developed the northern area as a region for providing furs, and they are also interested in the fisheries off the coast of Newfoundland. The French are trying to establish a dominant position in the north, with the help of the French government, which even ships out wives to the colonists. These ships are eagerly sought after by pirates. In 1690 war broke out between the French and English colonists.

Recently the French have expanded their interests to the area to the west of the Indian Line. They have established a number of forts along the Ohio river: there are signs that these will be fortified along the lines of those on the St Lawrence river. The French are mainly traders, so that they are usually on good terms with the Indians, although trouble has occurred, such as the 1689 Indian attack on Montreal. The French supply the Indians with weapons. The British, being settlers rather than traders, are interested in gaining land. The Indians are therefore more willing to join the French than the British. If the British settle to the West of the Indian Line, they may be faced with trouble from both the French and the Indians.

The area to the south of the British colonies is under the control of the Spanish, who are not a source of trouble at present.

References

Beacroft, BW and Smale, MA. *The Making of America,* Longman, 1972.
Currie, Barbara. *Pioneers in the American West,* Longman, 1969.
Gilbert, Martin. *American History Atlas,* Weidenfeld & Nicolson, 1968.
Kouwenhoven, JA. *The Columbia Historical Portrait of New York,* Doubleday, 1953.
Time Life. The British Empire. 1972.

5

Ironmaster

Ironmaster is a simulation designed for use at the eleven to eighteen age level. It is a role-play in which a pupil or pair of pupils identifies with a single firm of ironmasters. The simulation is carefully graded for difficulty, with Parts 1, 2 and 3 being especially suitable for the lower age or ability ranges; Parts 4 and 5 provide material for more advanced pupils.

The aim is to show stages in the development of the iron industry in the mid- and late-eighteenth century. The pupils are faced with a series of decisions about the type and location of furnaces, problems of financing, production, research etc.

The simulation is designed primarily for class use, with the firms of ironmasters in competition with each other to make the maximum profit. It can also be used for work with groups. The simulation will last for roughly six 40-minute periods.

Framework

The game

Each pair of pupils represents a firm of ironmasters which is already making

Historical actuality

The simulation is based on the Coalbrookdale Company. At the turn of the seventeenth century, Abraham Darby I

66

iron and brass pots and pans near the mouth of a major river.

By 1760 the firm has so prospered that it has saved £1,500 and decides to buy an inland furnace site to exploit the Midlands market for iron goods.

The choice of site will be influenced by the type of furnace used. The pupils have to decide between the coke and the charcoal processes.

Having decided on their method, the pupils choose a site for the new furnace. On Map 5, five possible sites are shown with the availability of raw materials: fuel (coke or charcoal), iron ore and limestone.

The pupils now embark on their first year's production. The decision on how much iron to make will be influenced both by costs and furnace capacity. Charcoal furnaces are limited to 200 tons of iron a year; coke furnaces to 300 tons.

(1677-1717) 'set on foot the Brass Works at or near Bristol' and 'attempted to mould cast Iron pots. . . in sand instead of Loam'.

In 1709 Darby moved from Bristol to Coalbrookdale in Shropshire to get nearer the expanding Midlands markets.

Although Darby pioneered coke smelting in the first decades of the eighteenth century, the method was not generally accepted until the late eighteenth century. In 1760 as many new charcoal as coke furnaces were built.

Map 5 is a mirror image of the Severn Valley. The sites shown were used by early ironmasters. Site B is Coalbrookdale where Darby 'took a lease of an old Blast Furnace. . . blow'd with wood charcoal.'

At 1760 wage levels, the wages bill allows for a force of some 20 workers and 2 managers. Iron ore and limestone were very cheap, but coke and charcoal were expensive as they had to be processed. In 1750 charcoal represented 60 per cent of the total cost of iron production.

Mid-eighteenth-century furnaces were relatively small: the average annual output from charcoal furnaces was some 250 tons a year in 1760.

The pupils have to raise a loan to cover the cost of the first year's production. They can borrow the money from a Bristol merchant at 5 per cent interest a year. Production can then begin.

At the end of the first year's production, the firm is told the price it has received for its iron. Worked iron from charcoal furnaces fetches £20 per ton; that from coke furnaces, £15 per ton. The firm's profit is then calculated and compared with that of other firms.

In Part 4 the game moves on to 1790. Each firm has done well and accumulated a capital of £5,500. There is therefore a move to expand furnace capacity. Map 6 shows possible new sites in the same region. In choosing, an important factor is access to coal mines, as technical improvements have led to the general adoption of the coke method of smelting.

Ironmasters were faced with problems of financing. Darby raised money from Bristol sources. The mid-eighteenth century rate of interest for commercial ventures was some 5 per cent p.a., slightly higher than government funds which yielded 3–4 per cent p.a.

Because of the large number of independent ironmasters, iron prices fluctuated according to demand. In 1765, pig iron fetched between £7 and £8 per ton (the higher price on the Sales card represents the price charged for bar iron and cast goods). Iron from charcoal furnaces was of a higher quality; John Roebuck's experiments to produce bar iron and steel with coke fuel in the 1760s were largely a failure.

The profit margins were high for a successful and progressive ironmaster: the capital of the Carron Works increased by nearly £140,000 between 1760 and 1774.

Map 6 shows the Coalbrookdale region, with Darby's original works at X. Sites B, C, D and E all had furnaces built on them: the bridge is the Iron Bridge, built in 1779; and the china works are those of the Coalport Company.

Closeness to coal mines was crucial: the price of coal doubled within five miles of the pithead. The use of coke fuel became more widespread: by 1790 there were eighty-one coke furnaces in blast in England, and only twenty-five using charcoal. Cort's puddling process of 1784 was the final technical break-through necessary for the mass production of high quality iron from coke furnaces.

The firm has to decide on the allocation of remaining capital between four areas: research into production methods; the building up of a sales organization; the hire of a steam engine; or keeping a cash reserve.

There was intense competition in the iron industry, and great efforts were made to improve production methods. The Coalbrookdale Company was actively engaged on research into the manufacture of bar iron. There was also the problem of sales: the iron industry was suffering from over-capacity right up to the rail age. From 1788-96 iron production doubled to 125,000 tons a year.

Originally, steam engines were used to pump water back into the mill pool after it had powered a water wheel. In 1776 John Wilkinson successfully applied a steam engine to the working of the bellows of his furnace at Willey, Shropshire. The hire of a Boulton & Watt steam engine was some £2,000 p.a.

To raise money for the firm's operations, the players issue sixteen shares in the firm.

It was usual eighteenth-century commercial practice to raise money for new business ventures by issuing shares, normally a few at high cost.

The firm completes production and is told the sale price of its iron. This price, plus additional information on the quantity of iron made and sold and its quality, determines the profit

In this period there were wide differences in price for different qualities of iron. In 1790 the Furness Iron Works sold pig iron for £8.10s per ton; in 1806-7 the minimum price for bar iron was £16 per ton; and a ton of steel cost £141.

69

level. Again the pupils compare their profits with those of their rivals.

Finally, the firm decides how to use its profits, choosing between reinvestment, paying a dividend, keeping a reserve etc.

Many of the most successful businesses were characterized by a high level of reinvestment, notably the Coalbrookdale Company and the Carron Works.

Equipment

Apart from the text, only pencils and erasers are needed.

Playing procedure

1. The class is divided into groups, pairs or individuals and a copy of the text is given to each pupil.

2. The text is read aloud down to Decision Table 5.1, and any difficult points elucidated by the teacher (for instance, the meaning of 'smelting'.)

3. The points for charcoal and coke as fuels can form the basis for a class discussion: alternatively, each 'firm' can discuss them separately. Before the firms fill in the 'Own mark' section on the table, it is best to work through a 'Class mark' for one or two points. (The Class mark is the mark with the largest number of supporters.) This will give the pupils a clear idea of how the 'scoring' works.

4. When all firms have chosen their method, it is useful to discuss the reasoning behind such decisions.

5. Part 2 is a location exercise based on a mirror image map of the Severn and its estuary. There should be few difficulties with Table 2, but it is best to work through one point for one site orally, to make certain that the scoring is understood. The Bonus sites are: B for coke furnaces; B or D for charcoal furnaces.

6. In Part 3 the procedure for filling in the Account sheet (1760) (Table 5.7) will need a fuller explanation than other parts of the simulation. It is important that as each item to go into the Account

70

sheet is mentioned it should be accurately filled in. With regard to the loan, it should be pointed out that this is long-term, so only the *interest* need appear in the Account sheet.

7. The Sales card (1760) on p.87, is read out and each firm can then calculate its profit: the most successful firm is then revealed. It will be found that those choosing the coke method have not necessarily done best: in 1760, charcoal was in many ways a more satisfactory fuel.

8. Part 4 is based on Coalbrookdale: the procedure is as for Part 2. 'Bonus sites' are all other than A, which is unsuitable in a number of ways.

9. Part 5 is the most complex of the simulation, and it is best to divide it into three sections:

(a) The investment of money.

(b) Costs of the year's production.

(c) The formation of a new company.

With younger pupils, a class discussion on investment possibilities (steam engines etc.) will be of help prior to each firm making its own decisions. A simple explanation of what a share is may be necessary; the advantages of selling shares, rather than raising a loan, can be discussed.

10. The Sales card (1790) on p.88 is distributed. Values of sales can be read off it, and profits worked out. Again, the most profitable firm can be identified and the reasons for success discussed on a class basis.

11. The final decision on what to do with the profit is open-ended: there is no exclusively correct answer.

Ironmaster

Part 1: Choosing a furnace

You and your partner are ironmasters. Your works consists of a furnace and a forge where the iron is worked into shape. The works is near a major port at the mouth of a large river. The main things your business makes and sells are iron and brass pots and pans.

Together you have saved £1,500 and you decide to use this money to buy a furnace at an inland site. This should help you to find new markets to sell your goods.

Table 5.1

	Own mark	Class mark
Charcoal: points in favour A. Charcoal is an old, well tried method and you will easily be able to hire skilled workmen to run a charcoal furnace.		
B. Charcoal furnaces produce a better quality iron than coke furnaces. This iron will fetch a higher price because it is easier to work in a forge than iron produced by the coke method.		
C. It should be easy to find a site for a charcoal furnace as wood is the fuel and there are still large areas of woodland.		
Total for charcoal		

The first problem is whether to buy a new furnace which burns *charcoal* or one that burns *coke* as a fuel. In 1709 the secret of smelt-iron by using coke was discovered at Coalbrookdale in Shropshire by Abraham Darby, who followed 'Dud' Dudley's experiments of the previous century. Now, in the year 1760, most people know of the coke method.

This coke method looks hopeful, but most ironmasters still use the charcoal method which must therefore have some advantages. To help you in the difficult choice between charcoal and coke Table 5.1 above sets out the advantages of both. Use the table and, by giving

Table 5.1 cont/d..

	Own mark	Class mark
Coke: points in favour D. You can have a coke furnace very near to a forge. With a charcoal furnace, the forge may have to be up to twenty miles away as both the furnace and the forge use a great deal of charcoal, so both must be surrounded by a large area of woodland.		
E. Coke can be produced quickly and will be available all the year round: whereas charcoal furnaces only work about half the year (owing to time spent collecting wood and making charcoal).		
F. Coke furnaces produce a greater quantity of iron than charcoal furnaces, up to one-third more iron a year.		
Total for coke		

marks of 5 as set out in the list below, show how important you think each method is:

Very important	5
Important	4
Quite important	3
Not very important	2
Unimportant	1

When you have decided how many marks to give for one of the points, write the mark down in Table 5.1 opposite the point. Use the

Map 5

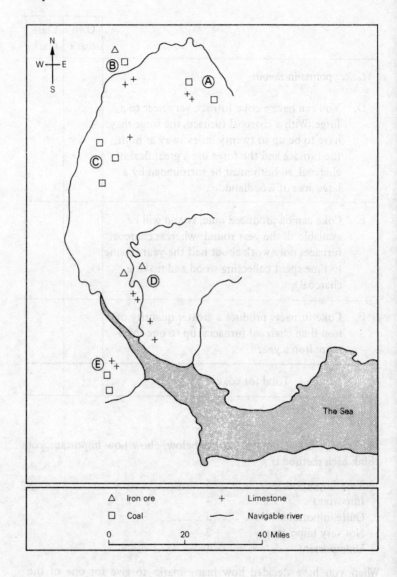

△	Iron ore	+	Limestone
□	Coal		Navigable river

0   20   40 Miles

column headed 'Own mark'. When you have put all the marks down, add up the total for charcoal and then the total for coke. Choose the method with the higher total marks.

Part 2: Choosing a site

You have decided to buy a .... furnace with the £1,500. Next you have to choose a suitable site for it.

The three things you will need to produce iron are limestone, iron ore and *either* charcoal (made from wood) *or* coke (made from coal.)

Look at Map 5. On this are five possible sites (A, B, C, D and E). Work out how well each of these sites fits the following points:

1. Nearness to limestone quarries.
2. Closeness to iron ore mines.
3. Nearness to a river so that the iron goods can be taken in barges to a forge, or to nearby towns for sale. (It is very difficult to move heavy goods by road at this time.) All the rivers shown on Map 5 are suitable for barges.
4. (*for coke furnaces only*). Closeness of the furnace site to coal mines. (This point does not concern you if you have a charcoal furnace, as all the sites are in wooded areas which will provide fuel.)

For each point, give each site a mark out of 5 according to the following scale:

Very good   5
Good   4
Fair   3
Poor   2
Bad   1

Write the marks in the correct boxes in Table 5.2. Then add up the total marks for each site.

75

Table 5.2. Furnace site

Site	A	B	C	D	E
Point 1					
2					
3					
(Coke only) 4					
Totals					

You can now list the sites in order of suitability in Table 5.3, putting the best one first. (If two sites have equal marks, the one nearer the sea will be better, as this will make it easier to ship goods for sale overseas.)

Table 5.3. Site choice for a . . . . furnace

Choice	1st	2nd	3rd	4th	5th
Site					

Site Bonus 1

The bonus sites will now be read out. If you have chosen a bonus site for your type of furnace, tick the box 'Site Bonus 1'. A bonus site will save your money later on.

Part 3: First year's production

After buying a furnace, you can begin your first year's production of iron. You know that iron pots and pans will sell for an average of about £15 a ton, and the price may go up as there is a war on. Your problem is to work out how much your costs of production will be, as you will have to raise money to pay for these costs.

You will have the following fixed costs to pay, whichever type of furnace you choose:

Wages for skilled workmen: £600
Equipment and forge   :   £300

Turn to your Account sheet (1760) (Table 5.7) and write in the above figures in the *debit* column opposite the first two items.

Next comes the cost of raw materials. Iron ore and limestone (mixed together) costs £1 for 10 tons: coke or charcoal costs £25 for 10 tons. Below is a cost table which shows you how much you will have to pay for raw materials to produce various tonnages of iron.

Table 5.4. Cost of raw materials

Iron Production	Iron ore and limestone	Cost	Coke or charcoal	Cost
100 tons	300 tons	£30	300 tons	£ 750
150 tons	450 tons	£45	450 tons	£1,125
200 tons	600 tons	£60	600 tons	£1,500
250 tons	750 tons	£75	750 tons	£1,875
300 tons	900 tons	£90	900 tons	£2,250

Now you must decide how much iron you want to produce. Consider the following points:

1. In one year, a *charcoal* furnace can produce up to 200 tons of iron: a *coke* furnace can produce up to 300 tons of iron.
2. You need not produce the maximum tonnage for your type of furnace. If you make a loss on iron production this year, the loss should be smaller if the tonnage is small.
3. However much iron you produce, you will still have to pay £900 for the labour force, the equipment and the forge. Thus if you

77

produce a small tonnage of iron, it will cost you more per ton to make than for a large tonnage, where the cost of £900 will be spread over more tons.

You decide to produce . . . . tons of iron. From Table 5.4 find the cost of the iron ore and limestone, and the coke or charcoal you will need. Write these sums in the *debit* column of the Account sheet (1760) (Table 5.7). Now, using Table 5.5, add up your debit so far:

Table 5.5

Wages, equipment etc.	£ 900
Iron ore and limestone	£
Coke or charcoal	£
Total	

This total is the amount of money you will have to raise.

A Bristol merchant will lend you this money if you pay him 5 per cent interest on the loan at the end of the year. He will lend you one of the following sums, shown in Table 5.6 under 'Loan':

Table 5.6

Loan	5% interest on loan
£2,100	£105
£2,500	£125
£2,900	£145
£3,300	£165
£3,700	£185

Choose the smallest loan which will cover your costs. (If you choose a much larger loan, you will have to pay unnecessary interest at the end of the year.)

You can now go into production and make the . . . . . . tons of iron you intended. The Sales card (1760) will be issued and read out. Find out the selling price of the type and amount of the iron you have produced, and enter this sum in the credit column of the Account sheet (1760) (Table 5.7 below).

If you chose a bonus site (see page 70), you can write down '£300' opposite 'Site Bonus 1' in the *credit* column, as this is what you saved on production costs over the year as a result of picking a good site for your furnace.

You can now pay the interest on the loan (see Table 5.6 above); so enter this sum in the *debit* column of the Account sheet (1760) opposite 'Loan interest at 5 per cent'.

Table 5.7. Account sheet (1760)

Credit	£	Debit	£
Value of sales		Skilled workmen	
Site Bonus 1		Equipment & forge	
		Iron ore & limestone	
		Charcoal or coke	
		Loan interest at 5%	
Total credit		Total debit	

Now add up the *credit* column and write the result by 'Total credit'. Then add up the *debit* column and write the result by 'Total debit'.

To find out how successful you have been, write the sums for 'Total credit' and 'Total debit' in Table 5.8. Subtract the *debit* from the *credit*.

Map 6

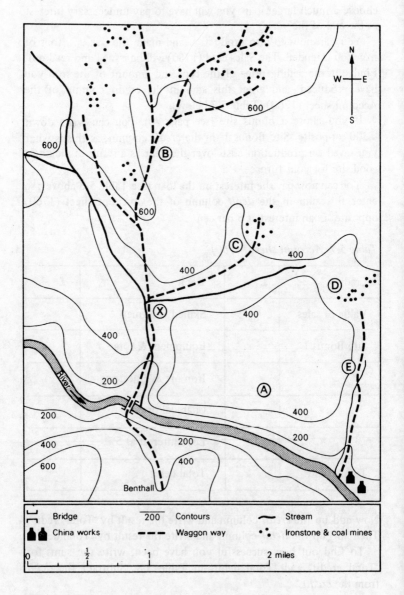

Legend:
- Bridge
- China works
- 200 Contours
- Waggon way
- Stream
- Ironstone & coal mines

0   ½   1   2 miles

Table 5.8. Profit or loss (1760)

Total credit	
Total debit	
Result	

In 1760, I/we made a *profit/loss* of £ . . . .

Signed . . . .

. . . .

Part 4: A new furnace site

We now move on thirty years to 1790. Your firm has traded success-fully, and built two new furnaces on the old site. You have made a profit of £5,500, which includes all previous trading. Write this sum in the *credit* column of the Account sheet (1790) (Table 5.14). A fourth and larger furnace is now needed as there has been a great increase in demand for improved pig iron for all uses in forges.

You have decided to concentrate on the coke method (which is improved) and the furnace will cost £1,500. Place this sum in the *debit* column of the Account sheet (1790) opposite 'Cost of furnace'. You will have to find a new site for this furnace, as the old site is now too crowded.

The area for a new site is shown on Map 6. The old works is at site X. The new works, which will include a forge, could be sited at A, B, C, D or E. To make your choice, consider the following points. As for previous tables, give a mark out of 5 for each point according to suitability, and enter the marks in Table 5.9.

1. Nearness to ironstone and coal mines. A group of eight mines will keep a furnace supplied. (Each dot on Map 6 represents one mine.)

81

2. Closeness to the Benthall limestone quarries, which are to the south of the river. They can be reached by the toll bridge.
3. Position downhill from the ironstone and coal mines, so that the loaded waggons can freewheel on rails down to the furnace site.
4. Closeness to the river front, where the finished iron goods can be loaded for shipping. Note that only the main river is navigable.

Table 5.9. Site for a new furnace and forge

Site	A	B	C	D	E
Point 1					
2					
3					
4					
Totals					

The site with the highest total marks will be the best. Enter the sites in order of suitability in Table 5.10. below:

Table 5.10

Choice	1st	2nd	3rd	4th	5th		Site Bonus 2
Site							

The bonus site will now be read out. If you have chosen a bonus site for the new furnace, tick the box 'Site Bonus 2'. A bonus site will save you money later on.
82

Part 5: Business section

You have chosen the new furnace site and can now decide how to spend the remaining £4,000 from your profits. There are four possible uses for this money. You can spend it on *all* the ideas (numbered 1—4 below) or *some* of them, or only *one*. The ideas are as follows:

1. *Research to improve methods of production.* Research might enable you to discover a much cheaper method of making pig iron into bar iron (for use in the forge).
2. *Building up a sales organization to distribute and sell the iron.* Money spent on hiring agents might mean that the firm could sell more of its iron than at present. After the War of American Independence (1775-83), the price of iron dropped, and since then it has been difficult to sell large quantities of iron.
3. *Hiring a steam engine from Boulton and Watt.* Use of a steam engine would increase your output by half as much again. The engine would be used to work the bellows of the furnace. At present a water-wheel is normally used for this, but in summer the water level in the mill dam is sometimes too low to work the wheel.
4. *Keeping a reserve of money.* You could keep all or part of the £4,000 to help cover any loss which you might make on the year's production.

A steam engine costs £2,000 to install. You may spend greater or smaller amounts of the money (in multiples of £500) on any other projects. (Note that only *one* steam engine is needed for your new furnace.)

When you have decided about ideas 1, 2, 3 and 4, write down the amounts to be spent on each in the *debit* column of the Account sheet (1790) (Table 5.14). If you are keeping a reserve of money, this need not be entered as it is part of the £5,500 already entered in the *credit* column.

You now have to work out your basic production costs. The largest cost will be raw materials (you know that the furnace must work at full capacity for the greatest potential profit.) Table 5.11 below shows the amounts of iron you expect to produce either *with* or *without* a steam engine. It also shows the tonnages of raw materials (iron ore mixed with limestone, and coke) which you will need, and their cost:

Table 5.11 Cost of raw materials

	Expected output	Iron-ore and limestone	Coke
With steam engine	1,200 tons	3,600 tons (£360)	3,600 tons (£4,500)
No steam engine	800 tons	2,400 tons (£240)	2,400 tons (£3,000)

Enter the cost of your raw materials in the *debit* column of the Account sheet (1790). You will also have to enter the cost of the new furnace (£1,500) and the following sums in the *debit* column:

Skilled labour	£800
Equipment	£600

You will have to raise money to pay for all this. To find out how much is needed, add up your debit so far, using Table 5.12.

Table 5.12. Debit so far

Projects (research etc.)	
Labour and equipment	
Furnace	
Raw materials	
Total	

The sum in your *credit* column is £5,500, so subtract this from the *debit* total so far, and that will show you how much money you have to raise. Use Table 5.13 for this.

Table 5.13. Loan required

Debit	£
Credit	£
Result	£

Next you have to raise the money. You do this by forming a company for the new furnace, and then selling shares in the company. These shares will be bought by local landowners, other ironmasters and Bristol merchants. There will be sixteen shares, of which you will keep six. These represent your share in the business. The remaining ten shares will each cost one-tenth of the money you have to raise.

Each share in the company therefore costs £ . . . .

You can now go into production. The Sales card (1790) will be given out. How well you have done will depend on how you spent your money on the four projects. There are two things you will have to work out:

1. What *tonnage* of iron you managed to sell (see Table 5.17), on the Sales card (1790).
2. What *price* per ton you have sold that iron for (see Table 5.18), on the Sales card (1790).

When you have found out how much you have made from selling your iron, enter this sum in the *credit* column of the Account sheet (1790) opposite 'Value of sales'. Also in the *credit* column, enter £300 opposite Site Bonus 2 if you gained a site bonus in Part 4.

Table 5.14 Account Sheet (1790)

Credit	£	Debit	£
Trading profit		Cost of furnace	
Value of sales		Research	
Site Bonus 2		Sales organization	
		Hiring steam engine	
		Iron ore + limestone	
		Coke	
		Skilled labour	
		Equipment	
Total credit		Total debit	

Now add up the *credit* column, and then add up the *debit* column.
To discover how well you have done, write the sums for Total credit
and Total debit in Profit and Loss Table 5.15 below. Subtract the
debit from the *credit*.

Table 5.15. Profit and loss (1790)

Total credit	£
Total debit	£
Result	£

If you have made a profit, you will have to decide what to do with the money. There are several possibilities:

1. You could share the profit among all the shareholders, including yourself. The investors would expect a dividend from their investment, and so might feel a lack of confidence in your firm if they did not get one. Also, a dividend would encourage new investors if you decide to raise capital to expand your works in the future.
2. You could reinvest all the profits in the firm. This might mean an improvement could be made to the quality or quantity of your iron production, or both. This might lead to a far larger profit next year, as you will have learnt from your previous errors over investing money in the four projects.
3. You could keep all or part of the profits as a reserve against a possible loss in future trading.
4. You could share a proportion of the profits among the shareholders, and keep the rest either for reinvestment in the firm, or as a reserve, or both.

Discuss the above possibilities with your partner. When you have reached an agreement, note your decision, giving reasons for your choices.

Sales Card (1760)

The increase in production owing to the spread of the coke method has caused a surplus of iron. Prices for iron and iron goods produced by *coke* furnaces have therefore not gone up, but have remained the same at *£15 per ton.*

Iron from charcoal furnaces is in high demand owing to its excellent quality, and it can be sold for *£20 per ton.*

Using Table 5.16 you can find out how much the amount of iron you made will sell for:

Table 5.16. Value of sales

Tons of iron produced	Coke furnaces Total value at £15 per ton	Charcoal furnaces Total value at £20 per ton
100 tons	£1,500	£2,000
150 tons	£2,250	£3,000
200 tons	£3,000	£4,000
250 tons	£3,750	-
300 tons	£4,500	-

Sales Card (1790)

During most of the eighteenth century, more iron was produced than was sold. Look at Table 5.17 below to find out how much iron you made and sold:

Table 5.17. Tonnage of iron sold

	Money spent on sales organization			
	£1,000 or less	£1,500 or £2,000	£2,500 or £3,000	£3,500 or £4,000
With steam engine	1,000 tons	1,000 tons	—	—
No steam	600 tons	700 tons	750 tons	775 tons

Table 5.18. Value of sales

		Tons of iron sold					
		600	700	750	775	1,000	1,100
Money used on research	Price of iron per ton						
£1,500 or less	£7	£4,200	£4,900	£5,250	£5,425	£ 7,000	£7,700
£2,000 or more	£14	£8,400	£9,800	-	-	£14,000	-

The *selling price* of your iron per ton will depend on how much you spent on research. If you spent £1,500 or less, your iron will not be improved in quality: you therefore have to sell it for the normal *pig iron* price of *£7 per ton*. If you spent £2,000 or more, you managed to produce *bar iron* which can be easily worked in a furnace and therefore sells at *£14 per ton*.

Table 5.18 on the previous page shows the total value of sales of the tonnage of iron you made, according to how much you spent on research.

References

Beales, HL. *The Industrial Revolution, 1750-1850,* Longman, 1928.

Fell, A. *The Early Iron Industry of Furness and District,* Cass, 1968.

Hartwell, RM (ed). *The Causes of the Industrial Revolution in England,* Methuen, 1967.

Hobsbawm, EJ. *Industry and Empire,* Weidenfeld & Nicolson, 1969.

Lord, J. *Capital and Steam-Power, 1750-1800,* Cass, 1966.

Mitchell, BR. *Abstract of British Historical Statistics,* 1962.

Musson, AE and Robinson, E. *Science and Technology in the Industrial Revolution,* Manchester University Press, 1969.

Nef, JU. *The Rise of the British Coal Industry,* Cass, 1966.

Raistrick, A. *Dynasty of Iron Founders,* Longmans, 1953.

Schubert, HR. *History of the British Iron and Steel Industry c. 450 B.C. to A.D. 1775,* Routledge, 1957.

6

Village Enclosure

Village Enclosure is a simulation containing location exercises, decision tables and class, group and individual role-play exercises. It is designed for the nine to sixteen years age range.

The simulation is set around the year 1800 and aims to show changes that occurred in a typical village during the switch from the essentially medieval 'open-field' system of farming to the modern enclosed pattern. Pupils identify with various characters, from the Enclosure Commissioners to the squatters, thus deepening their understanding of the motivation of the personalities concerned, and the changes resulting from the Enclosure movement.

It is recommended that in class the pupils work in pairs and that they discuss the decisions they take. There is provision for a class debate, if desired. The four parts of the simulation take approximately five 40-minute periods to complete.

Framework

Game	*Historical actuality*
Map 7 shows a typical medieval open-field system. The pupils have to decide where would be the	At the end of the eighteenth century the medieval farming pattern remained in large areas of central England, particularly in the grain growing areas

best site on the map for their village, which has had to be moved owing to pressure from a great territorial magnate.

of the Midlands. Many of these villages had been partly enclosed, but Laxton still survives with its medieval pattern intact.

With the widespread building of country houses and the landscaping of their surrounds, villages could be moved to new sites, as at Atcham in Shropshire.

Each pupil takes the part of one of fourteen villagers, ranging from the Squire who owns twenty-four strips, to a Small Freeholder who owns two strips. There are also some squatters who have taken illegal smallholdings from the common land.

The occupational structure of the pre-enclosure village ranged from the yeoman to the peasant. In addition, there would be a range of village craftsmen: this enabled the village to be relatively self-sufficient. Because of the increase in population from the 1740s, the problem of squatters increased; many of these were relatives of the villagers who had made clearings in the local woods or on the edge of commons.

Each pupil has to decide if enclosure would be of benefit to him, depending on his 'character' (shown in 'Notes on village characters'). There are various reasons for enclosure: more land could be cultivated; holdings could be consolidated; new machinery and techniques could be introduced. There are also reasons against enclosing: the squatters would be turned off the common; enclosure will be expensive; the Commissioners may be

Enclosure was becoming widespread by the late eighteenth century. The dissemination of ideas associated with the agricultural revolution, and the rise in grain prices, made enclosure increasingly attractive to farmers wishing to benefit from the markets which were opening up in the industrial centres. The breakthrough in transport with the increase in turnpikes and the 'canal mania' of the 1790s made the transport of surplus agricultural produce increasingly profitable.

While enclosure benefited the more prosperous section of the community, it could operate against the interests of the smaller farmers: from being an

92

biased in favour of the Squire when they redistribute the land.

independent peasantry, they were likely to be turned into landless labourers. One reason was that the cost of getting an Enclosure Act passed and the subsequent work of the Commissioners, resulting in hedging and ditching, often proved ruinous. Such Commissioners were normally drawn from the same social stratum as the Squire.

The class holds a village meeting to debate these matters. If the owners of four-fifths of the land are in favour of enclosure, they will get an Enclosure Bill put before Parliament.

After the 1801 Enclosure Act, enclosure decisions had to be agreed to by owners of four-fifths of the village land. If such agreement was reached, the local borough or county M.P.s would be approached to put the measure forward.

After three years, an Enclosure Act has been passed. The pupils now take the part of Enclosure Commissioners. On Map 8, they redistribute the land among the villagers in proportion to their previous strip holdings. In doing so, they should tend to give the best of the new land to the larger landowners, who are near to them in class and interests.

The first decade of the nineteenth century saw the peak of the enclosure movement. Once an Enclosure Act had been passed (and it might be delayed), Commissioners were appointed to apportion the land between the various freeholders.

Typical of such appointments were those at Findern in 1780 and Twyford in 1844, both in Derbyshire.

With the help of a professional surveyor, the Commissioners would allocate the land and the results would be outlined on the enclosure award and its associated map. The distribution of the land normally favoured the larger landowners, particularly the local gentry, who would closely associate with the Commissioners.

93

The pupils move on a further ten years. On Map 9 they draw in various changes that have occurred. The main freeholders have bought up and incorporated the holdings of the small freeholders, who have had to sell up to pay for the cost of the enclosure and have now become landless labourers.

The enclosure of a village was followed by a radical change in the pattern of settlement. The small landowners were forced to sell holdings to meet the costs of enclosure and they either became landless labourers, or left the district and drifted to the new manufacturing towns.

The pupils also have to decide the best place for some of the larger freeholders to build farm houses on their new consolidated holdings, and where the tracks to these farms should run.

Enclosure was normally followed by the break up of the medieval nucleated village. The freeholders moved from the centre of the village and built on their new holdings – as at Eggington, Derbyshire. The larger freeholders built extensive farm complexes.

Finally the pupils compare Map 9 'Final results of enclosure' with Map 7, 'Before enclosure'.

Equipment

Pencils, erasers, and tracing paper (if available).

Playing procedure

1. The class is divided into individuals, pairs or groups and each pupil is given a copy of the text.
2. When the text has been read aloud down to Table 6.1, and Map 7 studied, Point 1 for Site A should be attempted. The mark supported by the majority of the class is then entered under 'Class result'. Further class results may be worked through if desired.

94

3. When each pair/group has completed all its 'Own result' columns, and decided on a site, the rest of the class results can be filled in. Differences between these and individual results can form the basis for a class discussion.

4. In Part 2, the pairs/groups are allocated roles 1–14 as shown in Table 6.2. Each role should be filled, and no role duplicated (e.g. there should not be two Squires). Any extra groups can take the the role of squatters.

5. The pupils then look at the Information sheet of Village characters: this will help fix their own attitudes and warn them of the probable attitudes of other villagers. They then read through Table 6.3, assessing how the various factors will affect them.

6. The enclosure decision (Table 6.4) can take the form of a class debate, with the spokesman for each character stating a view in turn. At the end, each character states whether he is for or against enclosure, and decisions are registed in Table 6.4.

7. For Part 3, if the village decided *not* to enclose, it should be pointed out that nearly every village did eventually enclose (Laxton is a rare exception). In the land allocation pupils must accept that enclosures will tend to be biased in favour of the large landowners.

8. Table 6.5 is designed as an analysis table to check that the allocation of land was realistic. Any high scores low on the list should be examined.

9. In Part 4, the re-allocation of the Small Freeholders' land will be easiest if their number is crossed out on Map 8 and that of the new owner substituted. This will make transference to Map 9 simpler.

10. The final question implies that improvements extended beyond the limits of the enclosed fields.

Village Enclosure

Part 1

Map 7 'Before enclosure' shows the open-field pattern of a typical pre-enclosure village. There are three main fields and a common, which borders the north-eastern field.

The area on the map adjoins the estates of a great landowner (such as the Duke of Newcastle who had estates in Nottinghamshire).

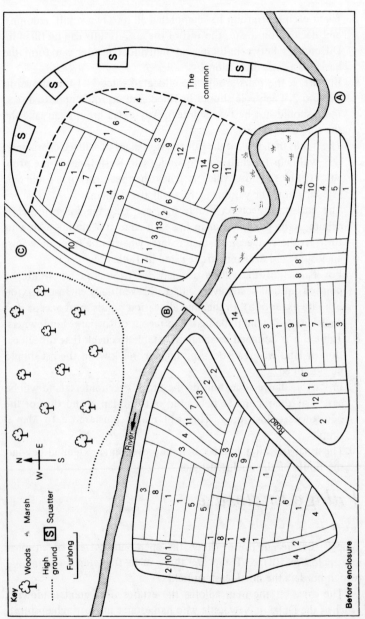

Map 7

Before enclosure

The great landowner has in this case decided to landscape his large estates, and has employed the famous landscape gardener, Capability Brown, who suggests that one of the villages should be moved. Possible positions for a new site are marked A, B and C on Map 7.

Although the great landowner does not own the village, he is willing to pay for the cost of moving and rehousing the villagers. He has so much influence over the Squire of the village and the other inhabitants that he has been able to persuade them to move to one of the new sites.

The first problem is to try to decide which of the new sites for the village would be best. The five most important points for a good site are:

1. Nearness to the common, on which all the owners of the land are allowed to graze their cattle and sheep.
2. Nearness to the strips in the three fields.
3. Nearness to the wood, where the pigs can feed; the wood also provides timber for building and for fuel.
4. Nearness to the stream, which provides water for homes (for drinking, washing and cooking) and for pigs, sheep and cows.
5. Nearness to the road.

Now look at Map 7. Try to judge how well each site does on each of the points 1–5. Give a mark out of 10 for each point: if a site does well for a point, give it 9 or even 10 out of 10; if it does badly, give it 2 or 3 out of 10.

Table 6.1. Village choice

Point	Site A		Site B		Site C	
	Own result	Class result	Own result	Class result	Own result	Class result
1						
2						
3						
4						
5						
Total						

Part 2

The three main fields of the village are divided up into strips, numbered 1–14, which belong to the landholders of the village. For example, the strips numbered '1' belong to the Squire, while those numbered '11' belong to a Small Freeholder. Table 6.2 shows who are the landholders and the amount of land they own:

Table 6.2

Number	Owner	Quantity of strips
1	The Squire	24
2	The Rector (Vicar)	8
3	Yeoman	8
4	Yeoman	8
5	Freeholder	4
6	Freeholder	4
7	Freeholder	4
8	Freeholder	4
9	Freeholder	4
10	Freeholder	4
11	Small Freeholder	2
12	Small Freeholder	2
13	Small Freeholder	2
14	Small Freeholder	2

The squatters, who have made clearings and built shacks on the edge of the common, do not concern us as they have no legal right to their land and so are not included above.

When you have found out which is your number, look up about that person under 'Village characters' (p. 108). Try to look at things from his point of view.

The enclosure decision

The year is 1810. The Squire, Vicar and two Yeomen have called a parish meeting in the church to discuss whether to enclose the village's common fields and common. Table 6.3 below shows some of the points for and against enclosure. You have gone to the meeting, and now you have to decide whether you are for or against enclosure.

Remembering your character, look carefully at Table 6.3, and try to work out if enclosure will be to your advantage. Also look at where your strips are at present (see Map 7).

Table 6.3

A. With enclosure, more land can be cultivated. At present one field is left fallow (uncultivated) each year. If the land is enclosed, all of it including the common, could be farmed.

B. Each farmer's land could all be in one place. This would encourage the use of modern farming methods and machinery.

C. Many agricultural improvements could be made, for instance:

   1. Land could be drained.
   2. Animals and crops could be separated from those of other farmers by hedges and ditches. This would cut down the spread of disease and weeds.
   3. New and improved crops could be grown, and it would also be possible to improve the breeding of animals. Both these things are difficult at present.

D. The squatters will be turned off the common. They are related to some of the Freeholders and Small Freeholders.

E. The cost of enclosing the land (including hedging, ditching and road-building) will be so expensive that the Small Freeholders will almost certainly have to sell their land to pay these costs.

continued overleaf...

F. It is known that the Enclosure Commissioners (the men who divide up the common fields and the common among landholders) usually favour large landowners. This means that the Freeholders and Small Freeholders will probably get poor land in place of their strips.

When you have decided whether you are in favour of enclosure or against it, announce your decision to the meeting and give your reasons. Make your announcement when asked.

As the decisions are announced, put a tick by those landholders in favour of enclosure, and a cross by those against. Use Table 6.4 for this.

When Table 6.4 is completed, cross out the number of strips of all those *against* enclosure. Then add up the total number of strips of those in *favour* of enclosure.

After the Act of Parliament of 1801, if this number is four-fifths of the total (in this case sixty-four strips or more) the village can enclose. The Squire can then approach Parliament for an Enclosure Act for the village, which will be automatically granted.

If the owners of *64 or more strips* wish to enclose, the village will enclose; if less, it will not enclose.

Village decision: The village will / will not enclose.

Part 3

It is now 1813. There has been a continued rise in the price of corn, which can be more profitably grown on enclosed land, so the village is clearly in favour of enclosure. The Squire has managed to get a local Enclosure Act through Parliament, and the village land can now be enclosed. He has managed this through his friendship with the two Members of Parliament for the county and through the work of his lawyer who lives in the county town.

As the Act has been passed, three Commissioners have been chosen. They will carry out a survey of the village land so that the open fields and the common land can be reorganized. The Commissioners are great landowners and friends of the Squire, so they stay with him at the manor house. They therefore make certain that the Squire gets the best choice of the village land, which has been divided into plots

Table 6.4 Enclosure decision

Landholder		For or against enclosure	Number of strips
1.	The Squire		24
2.	The Rector		8
3.	Yeoman		8
4.	Yeoman		8
5.	Freeholder		4
6.	Freeholder		4
7.	Freeholder		4
8.	Freeholder		4
9.	Freeholder		4
10.	Freeholder		4
11.	Small Freeholder		2
12.	Small Freeholder		2
13.	Small Freeholder		2
14.	Small Freeholder		2
Total number of *strips* of those in favour of enclosure:			

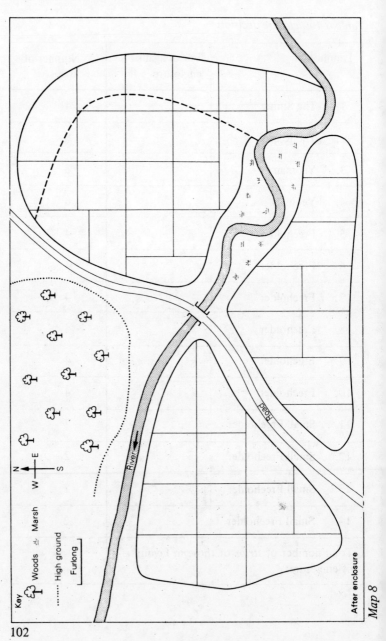

Key
🌲 Woods   ☖ Marsh

····· High ground

Furlong

N
W — E
S

After enclosure

Map 8

(as on Map 8). The Squire supports the interests of the Rector and the two Yeomen, and sees that they get favourable treatment.

Imagine that you are one of the Commissioners. You now have to share out all the village land. Use Map 8, 'After enclosure', to help you. Each plot shown is about one-fortieth of the area of the village land. A list of the number of plots to be given to each landowner is set out in Table 6.5.

Table 6.5. Number of new plots for each landholder

Owner	Number of new plots
1. The Squire	12
2. The Rector	4
3. Yeoman	4
4. Yeoman	4
5. Freeholder	2
6. Freeholder	2
7. Freeholder	2
8. Freeholder	2
9. Freeholder	2
10. Freeholder	2
11. Small Freeholder	1
12. Small Freeholder	1
13. Small Freeholder	1
14. Small Freeholder	1

Table 6.6

Landowner	A	B	C	D	E	Total
1. The Squire						
2. The Rector						
3. Yeoman						
4. Yeoman						
5. Freeholder						
6. Freeholder						
7. Freeholder						
8. Freeholder						
9. Freeholder						
10. Freeholder						
11. Small Freeholder						
12. Small Freeholder						
13. Small Freeholder						
14. Small Freeholder						

You have to give plots of land to each of the landowners in turn. Begin with the Squire, who will have twelve plots. Remember that those high on the list will get the best land. The following points A—E will help you decide which plots to give the various landowners:

A. Land in the old open fields is better for crops than the old common (the boundary of which is shown as a dotted line on Map 8).
B. The Squire, Rector and Yeomen would like their land to be near the village, where they have built large houses.
C. Most land owners would like all their land together to avoid unnecessary walking.
D. Land near the road is preferred as this makes it easy to move farm produce, machinery and cattle.
E. The area near the marsh often floods and the fields there become waterlogged and are poor for growing crops.

Show the plots which you have given to each landowner by marking them with the landowner's number.

In Table 6.6 opposite, give each landowner a mark out of 10 according to how his holding of new plots conforms to points A—E above. If his land does well according to a point, give it a high mark; if badly, give it a low mark.

Part 4

We now move on ten years after the Enclosure has been carried out. The Squire, Rector and Yeomen have kept their houses in the village, but the Freeholders have left their houses and moved to their new holdings.

Also, the Small Freeholders (who each had only one plot of land) found the cost of enclosure so great that they had to sell their plot to the Squire, Rector or Yeomen. In each case, the Small Freeholder's land goes to the landowner who is nearest to it. (When the Small Freeholder has two or more such neighbours, the land is sold to the one with the longest common boundary with the Small Freeholder's plot.) The Small Freeholders have now either become landless labourers or left the district.

On Map 9, 'Final results of enclosure', draw in the final field pattern after the Small Freeholders have sold their land. To do this: first

105

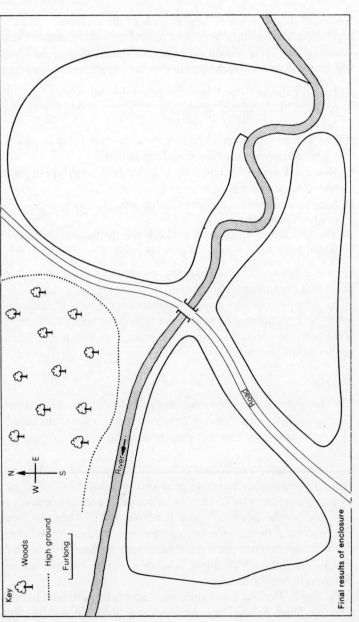

Key
Woods
High ground
Furlong

N E
W S
S

River

Road

Final results of enclosure

Map 9

change the number of the Small Freeholders' plots to that of the new owners; then use a sharp pencil or biro to draw over the boundaries of the new holdings (including land bought from the Small Freeholders) so that the outlines press through to Map 9. Then go over these in pencil.

The Freeholders are wondering whereabouts on their new holdings to build their houses. The factors they take into account are as follows. The house must be:

1. As near to the middle of the holding as possible.
2. Near to the main road.
3. Near to the stream, so that cattle can be easily driven there from the farm for water.

Now draw in small squares in each Freeholder's holding to show where his house and farm buildings are. The squares should be about the same size as those in Fig 6.1, below.

Fig. 6.1

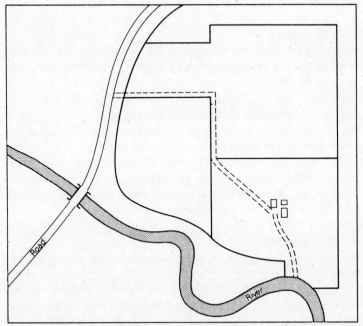

Then mark in the new tracks from each new farmhouse to the main road. Use double dashed lines for this, as in Fig. 6.1. You may also have to put in extra tracks so that cattle can easily reach the the stream.

Note that tracks can run along the boundary of any holding, but not *across* the land of another farmer. A number of farmers can share the same track, or part of a track.

Enclosure is now complete. To see some of the differences it has made to the village, compare Map 9, 'Final results of enclosure' with Map 9, 'Before enclosure'.

One final question: What happened to the marsh?

Village characters

Read through the following notes, which give a general idea of how villagers feel. Pay particular attention to the note which refers to your particular landholder. Numbers refer to those in Table 6.2.

1. The Squire

His strips are scattered throughout the three fields. He has been developing an increasing interest in new agricultural methods. The writings of the famous journalist Arthur Young in his *Annals of Agriculture* have particularly influenced him. This is sheep country and so he is interested in the selective breeding of sheep, following the experimental work of Robert Bakewell in Leicestershire in the 1760s. Selective breeding is now widespread.

At the County Quarter Sessions, the county races and at the market in the county town, he has discussed the new methods with other squires. Recently he saw an improved version of Jethro Tull's seed drill at an agricultural competition.

2. The Rector

His land, called the glebe, is in the poorest parts of the open fields. As a result, he has been having financial troubles owing to poor crops. These troubles have been made worse by the fact that he leads an active and costly social life. He goes fox-hunting with the Squire and several of the larger landowners. He pays a curate a very small sum of

108

money to carry out most of his religious duties. There is little sign that he has any interest in farming.

3. Yeoman

He is an old man, who believes in old-fashioned farming methods. As a young man in the 1750s, he saw the introduction of turnips and clover to provide winter feed for animals. At the time he approved of this 'Norfolk rotation' but now he believes that any further change will probably be for the worse. However, his sons are supporters of the new farming methods: they hope that these methods will enable the family to profit from the rise in grain prices which followed the renewal of war with France in 1803.

4. Yeoman

He is middle-aged and a progressive farmer. The county town is an expanding industrial centre, so there is a growing demand for meat. As a result, the Yeoman has been changing from purely arable farm-ing to sheep farming. His strip of land next to the common is used solely for grazing. Movable hurdles, called 'fleaks', are used to fence in his animals, which are also tethered to stop them straying. Recently he has spent a lot of money on having hurdles made. Also, he has just ploughed up two of his strips and put them down to clover. His only child, a daughter, is engaged to the eldest son of the other Yeoman — a marriage arranged when they were children.

5. Freeholder

Last year was a disaster for him. His crop of corn was first of all flattened in a storm, and then the Squire's sheep ate much of the rest of the crop when strong winds blew over the hurdles separating his land from the Squire's. He is unable to get compensation from the Squire because the legal case would cost him too much money. Consequently he has been forced to borrow money. He is very interested in new farming approaches, as he badly needs money to pay off his debts.

6. Freeholder

His strips are widely scattered. As he hurt his back in a farming acci-dent several years ago, he has trouble in moving about between the

109

different strips. He has concentrated on growing arable crops, in spite of the fact that many of his neighbours now think that more profit can be made out of sheep farming. One of his daughters is married to Freeholder 8, while his other daughter, who was the village beauty, ran away with the Squire's youngest son. As a result, Freeholder 6 and the Squire are not on speaking terms.

7. Freeholder

He is the most intelligent man in the village. He was educated at the small church school which the previous vicar built and left with enough money to employ a school dame. He is interested in current affairs, and on Friday nights he reads the county newspaper to the villagers in the local inn. He is well informed about the new agricultural methods, so he acts as a main source of information for the Small Freeholders. His own strips are widely scattered, and on different types of soil. In his experiments to grow new kinds of crops he has had only mixed success.

8. Freeholder

He is the only grazier in the village who has completely stopped growing arable crops. He has an agreement with the Vicar to rent strips in the South Field next to his own two, so he has been able to form a semi-enclosed field, surrounded by movable hurdles. His large flocks of sheep are poor specimens, and last year they suffered from foot-rot. He thinks this is because the bottom half of his enlarged field is waterlogged as it is so near the marsh.

9. Freeholder

He is the cousin of Freeholders 7 and 8, and is noted for his drunkenness. The strips he owns are poorly cultivated because he spends most mornings recovering from the effects of the previous evening in the ale house. Several times his wife and many children have had to apply to the parish for poor relief (money to buy food). The weeds on his land spread to neighbouring strips and cause a major problem to other farmers. Several farmers have tried to rent his strips from him, but he stubbornly refuses.

10. Freeholder

As a young man, he left the village to go and work in the new industries of the county town as he had an elder brother who would inherit the farm. However, his brother became drunk at the last election: while dancing on the parapet of the village's bridge, he fell into the stream and was drowned. His father died of heartbreak. The Freeholder returned and is full of ideas for introducing farming machinery into the village.

11. Small Freeholder

Last year, his land in the North Field was flooded and his crops there were ruined. He has a large family of twelve children, so he has had to accept poor relief and six of his children have entered the the workhouse. However, he has just hired two weaving frames from a manufacturer in the county town, and has got a good sum for his first load of cloth. Changes in the spinning industry have led to an increase in demand for cloth weavers, so he should be able to make good money. One of his sons has left home, and is a squatter on the common.

12. Small Freeholder

His wife is the sister of Freeholder 10, and his brother is married to the sister of Small Freeholder 13. He is an experienced farmer and is interested in the new farming approaches, but he thinks the cost of these would be a great burden on a Small Freeholder. He is regarded as the leader of the Small Freeholders. His strips are very far apart, but he is happy enough farming this scattered land.

13. Small Freeholder

Recently his wife died, and his children have all married and left home. He wishes to leave the village and work in the town for his brother, who owns a small spinning factory. However, his land is of very high quality: he manages to earn a comfortable living and has a small sum of money saved up. Although he knows about the new methods in farming, he is very happy to continue with the old methods, as he does not like change.

111

14. Small Freeholder

The soil on his strips is of low quality and he works only part-time as a farmer. He has great problems in protecting his crops as the hurdles round his land are very old and many of them are rotten. His neighbours' animals are constantly breaking through his fences and eating his crops. In order to make ends meet he has hired a weaving frame from a weaver in the county town. He keeps this frame in his cottage, and uses it when he is not farming. He is not interested in modern farming developments.

References

Addy, J. *The Agrarian Revolution,* Longman, 1972.

Cootes, RJ. *Britain Since 1700,* (Pictorial Education) Longman, 1972. *Pictorial Education,* June 1964.

Deane, P and Cole, WA. *British Economic Growth,* 1688-1959, Cambridge University Press, 1969.

Hoskins, WG. *The Making of the English Landscape,* Hodder & Stoughton, 1955.

Hoskins, WG. *Essays in Leicestershire History,* Liverpool University Press, 1950.

Patrick, AJ. *The Making of a Nation 1603-1789,* Penguin, 1967.

Quennell, M and CHB. *A History of Everyday Things in England,* Batsford, 1933.

University of Nottingham Manuscripts Department. *Laxton: Life in an Open Field Village.*

7

Trade and Discovery

The game produced here is intended for the nine to twelve years age range. It is the first part of a more complex simulation on sixteenth-century trading and exploration, showing many of the factors affecting English navigators and merchants in the period. The first part is based on Drake's circumnavigation of 1577-80.

It can be used as a class activity, with the pupils divided into groups of three or four. It is also suitable for separate group work, while others in the class are engaged on different projects. Part 1 should take two periods.

The game is designed to be flexible: it can be used as part of a line of development course (on exploration, or the ship), for a 'patch' on Elizabethan England, or as part of a chronological approach.

Framework

The game

The pupils take the role of one of Drake's captains in 1577. The maps on pages 118 and 119 show the world according to the current state of geographi-

Historical actuality

In November 1577 Drake sailed from Plymouth in the *Pelican,* with four other ships, intending a voyage of discovery round the world. Maps were becoming increasingly available, notably those of Lafreri and Ortelius.

113

cal knowledge. The wind arrows indicate trading winds.

The wind arrows are based on actual wind patterns at various seasons.

Each player has to sail his ship round the world. This fits in with the object of the voyage, an attack on the Spanish South American colonies from the west coast of South America, and the discovery of a great continent in the south.

Drake hoped that his fleet would be able to attack the Spanish settlements on the west coast of South America, as these were comparatively unprotected. He was also interested in discovering a southern continent, 'Terra Australis'.

On his turn, a pupil can move his ship a set number of squares. If the ship lands on a Chance square at the end of the turn, a spinner is used to discover what Chance number to refer to. The pupil then follows the relevant instructions.

Elizabethan sailing ships were still in an early stage of development as transoceanic transport. They were particularly vulnerable to chance hazards: the areas shown as Chance squares on the map were liable to be particularly difficult. Drake also faced problems on account of the novel nature of his voyage, and the hostilities between England and Spain.

The Chance sheet shows the range of problems which the player's ship may face.

Drake left Plymouth in November 1577, but by December he had only reached Falmouth, a few miles away, because of bad weather. In January 1578 he reached the west coast of Africa. At this point, Drake told his crews (166 men in all) that he intended to sail round the world. As no Englishman had ever done this, some of the seamen objected.

Chance number 2 deals with disputes on board. In Chance number 3, the ship is becalmed.

Drake sailed on towards South America, but his ships were becalmed.

Chance number 4 mentions the outbreak and crushing of a mutiny.

Then there was a mutiny led by Thomas Doughty. Drake landed south of Brazil, where he had to abandon two of his ships. He also dealt with Doughty, who was executed. In this place Drake found the remains of one of the men who had been on Magellan's voyage round the world over fifty years previously.

In Chance number 5 the ship is blown back by a storm.

It proved very difficult to sail round Cape Horn against the prevailing wind: only Drake's ship managed it. His two remaining ships were blown back, so they returned to England.

Chance number 6 shows some of the advantages of capturing an enemy vessel.

Once he was round Cape Horn (in November 1578) Drake looted an immense treasure of gold, silver and jewels from the Spanish colonies on the western side of South America. He also attacked and captured the Spanish galleon called *Cacafuego*, the cargo of which was worth over £10 million in modern money. It took three days to transfer all the treasure to Drake's ship. Drake sailed north as far as modern Vancouver, but as the weather was bad, in July 1579 he refitted his ship and set sail for the Spice Islands, reaching them in October 1580. At Ternate he bought 6 tons of spices.

Chance number 7 handles the problem of running aground.

Drake sailed on, and in December his ship (which had been renamed *Golden Hind*) went aground on a reef and Drake had to throw his best cannon and three tons of cloves overboard to to get the ship afloat again.

Chance number 8 states that scurvy has broken out and shows its effects.

In March 1580, at Java, Drake repaired the damage to his ship and sailed across the Indian Ocean. He arrived at the Cape of Good Hope in June, having had difficulty in sailing: disease left only a small number of sailors to man the ship.

Chance number 9 shows the benefits of favourable winds.

Once round the Cape, he found favourable winds and made good progress.

On 26 September 1580 he arrived back at Plymouth.

Chance numbers 10, 11 and 12 deal with general factors which were likely to affect early navigators.

Equipment

Each group will need a pair of scissors and a used matchstick (half for each spinner).

Note: (a) The teacher can provide dice (two per group) instead of the spinners.

      (b) The four ships per group can be cut out by the teacher beforehand (as can the spinners.)

      (c) The 'ships' will be more stable if each is impaled on a drawing pin.

Playing procedure

1. Divide the pupils into groups of four or less and issue each pupil with a copy of the text. Spinners (if required) and ships should be cut out.
2. It is strongly recommended that the Rules and Chance sheet should be read aloud, and any questions dealt with, before play begins.

Trade and discovery

Part 1

It is the year 1577. Many adventurers in England are interested in exploring the world (unknown coastlines are shown by the dotted lines on Map 10). You represent one of the captains of the ships which are going to sail with Sir Francis Drake on a voyage of discovery. Drake's ship, the *Pelican*, is at the head of a fleet of five small ships. Money for the voyage has been lent by Queen Elizabeth and a number of nobles.

At this time the Spanish have rich colonies in South America (around Area G on Map 10). They mine huge quantities of silver and send it back by ship to Spain. You hope to be able to capture some of these treasure ships. You also hope to discover a large southern continent known as 'Terra Australis'. The area where it is thought to be is marked on Map 11.

It is easiest to attack the Spanish colonies on the *western* side of South America where the large Spanish ships (galleons) have few guns, and their towns are only lightly defended. But Terra Australis is probably to the east of Africa. It will therefore be best to sail right round the world.

The object of the game is to sail from England (the 'England' square on Map 10) round the world and back to England again. This will mean passing from one side of the map to the other (see Rule 7). The first player to sail round the world and get back to England is the winner.

Rules

1. Up to four players can take part.
2. Cut out the numbered ships and the spinners. Push a used matchstick through the centre of the spinner. Each player uses the spinners, or throws the dice. The player with the highest number has his turn first, and takes the ship numbered 1. The player with the second highest number has the second turn, and takes ship No. 2, and so on.
3. Read through the Chance sheet for Part 1, so that you know what might happen if your ship finishes up on a Chance square at the end of your turn (see Rule 8).

Map 10

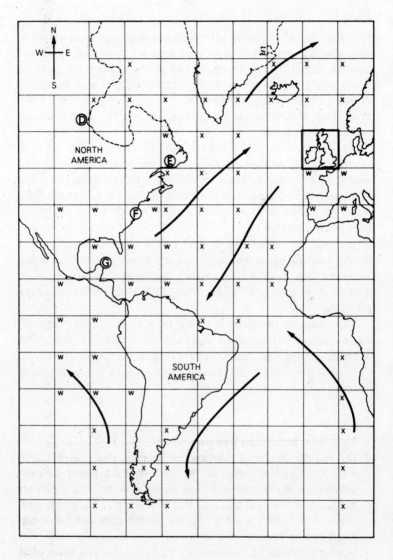

Note the lettered circles refer to trade/discovery areas for use in Part 2.

Map 11

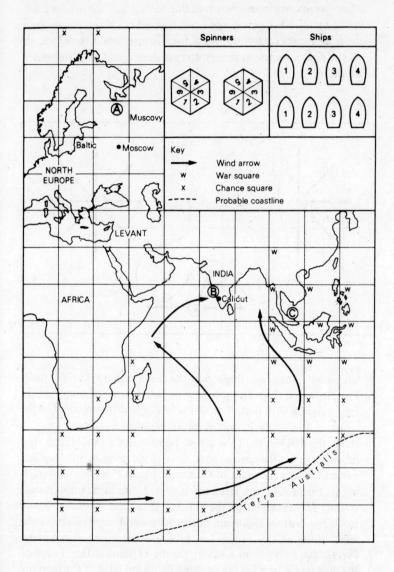

119

4. For his turn, a player has *three moves*. His ship can move three adjoining squares from where it is. But no ship may move over *land*. (as in Fig. 7.1.) A player need not take *all* his three moves for a turn, but moves cannot be 'saved' for a future turn. Fig. 7.1 shows all the directions which three different ships could go in *one move* of a turn.

Fig. 7.1

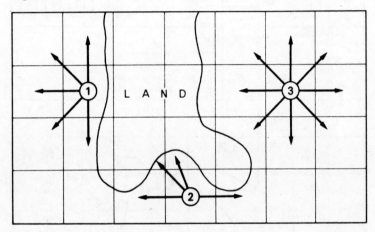

5. No more than *two* ships may be in a square at one time.
6. The arrows on the map show how the wind blows. If a ship moves into a square with part of an arrow in it, the ship can travel to the *point* of the arrow in *one* move. If the player does not want to travel the full length of the arrow, he need not do so. He can stop in any square the arrow goes through, as long as his ship has moved towards the point of the arrow. Fig. 7.2 shows a ship starting its turn in the top left hand corner. In its turn (three moves) it can, for example, go the full length of the wind arrow and reach the bottom righthand corner on move 3: or it can leave the wind arrow at any square (as shown) and reach another square.
7. Players can move from a square on the extreme lefthand edge of the map to a square on the extreme righthand edge of the map (or the other way round). This takes a full turn of three moves. The

Fig. 7.2

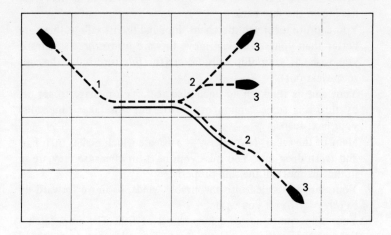

ship must stay on the same *row* of squares (counting from the bottom).

8. If a ship finishes its turn on a square marked 'x' (which shows a Chance square), the player uses the dice or the spinners and refers to the Chance sheet and obeys the instructions opposite the relevant number. (Squares marked 'w' count as Chance squares for Part 1.)

9. When it is his first turn, a player places his ship on the 'England' square and then takes his turn of three moves.

Chance sheet — Part 1

Numbers on the left refer to the totals of the dice or the spinners.

2. There is disagreement between you (the captain of the ship) and some of your officers, who are gentlemen adventurers; so you have to miss your next turn.

3. You miss your next turn because your ship is becalmed during a period when there are no winds.

4. There has been a mutiny on board. You miss your next turn, because you have to crush the revolt and hang the ringleaders. This causes delays.

5. Your ship has been caught in a sudden storm. Return it to the square where it stood at the beginning of this turn, as the storm has blown the ship back.

6. You capture a foreign merchant ship, and use its sails as these are better than yours. You can move forward up to *three* squares if you wish, as your ship sails faster (for *this* turn only: the sails soon wear out).

7. Your ship is stuck on an uncharted reef. You manage to get off by throwing some cannon overboard, but this takes time. Miss your next turn.

8. Many of the sailors have scurvy – a disease which makes their hair and teeth drop out. You miss your next turn because they are so ill they cannot sail the ship properly.

9. Your ship has sailed into favourable winds, so move forward up to *three* squares if you wish.

10. Your ship comes across a huge shoal of fish. The crew catch a large number of these, and have a feast. The sailors are strengthened and encouraged, so they work the ship better. Move forward up to *two* squares if you wish.

11. You capture a foreign ship with English prisoners on board. Go forward *two* squares, as these men add to your crew and enable your ship to sail faster.

12. The lookout reports seeing a sea-monster. This throws the crew into a panic, so you miss your next turn owing to the delays caused.

References

Corbett, JS. *Drake and the Tudor Navy,* Longmans, 1899.

Davies, RT. *The Golden Century of Spain, 1501-1621,* Macmillan, 1954.

Elton, GR. *England under the Tudors,* Methuen, 1955.

Hakluyt, R. *The Principal Navigations . . . ,* Macmillan, 1964.

Mattingly, G. *The Defeat of the Spanish Armada,* Cape, 1959.

Neale, JE. *Queen Elizabeth,* Cape, 1934.

Rowse, AL. *The Expansion of Elizabethan England,* Macmillan, 1955.

Unwin, R. *The Defeat of John Hawkins,* Penguin Books, 1962.

Williamson, JA. *The Age of Drake,* A & C Black, 1938.

8

The Russian Revolution

The Russian Revolution can be used either as a class or group role-play. It is designed for the fifteen to eighteen years age range. The simulation aims to illustrate the events in Russia from June to November, 1917. The players take the parts of different political groups during the Revolution: the Bolsheviks, Army commanders, Petrograd workers, and the Mensheviks and Social Revolutionaries. Each group has to attempt to form a government by making alliances with other parties around an agreed programme of aims. The simulation is of an in/out tray type, with a News Sheet announced at the beginning of each round to show changes in the situation. A round represents a period of four to six weeks. On the basis of the News Sheet and the programme of aims each party has adopted, negotiation can take place. The News Sheets are printed in chronological order, but need not necessarily be read out in this sequence.

About five 40-minute periods will be required for the simulation.

Framework

The game   *Historical actuality*

The pupils take the role of   After the March Revolution, five main
one of *five* groupings: the   groupings emerged in Petrograd, the

123

Bolsheviks; Liberals; Army commanders; Petrograd workers; Mensheviks and Social Revolutionaries. If the game is played as a group role-play, the pupils identify with whole parties; if on a class basis, they can take the role of individual characters. Possible roles which can be taken are shown in the Role Table (p.138). To help decide which party to adopt, the pupils read 'Parties in June 1917' (see p. 134) and work out the relative strength of the various groupings.

capital of Russia: the Bolsheviks; the Liberals; Army commanders; the workers; and the Mensheviks and Social Revolutionaries. The situation was extremely confused, with different elements jockeying for power.

The Petrograd situation in June 1917 is similar to that described in 'Parties in June 1917'.

During this period it was hard to gauge the relative strengths of the parties, not least because of fluidity between them: Kerensky (the Liberal leader) was originally a major figure in the Petrograd Soviet.

Each party decides on its political aims from the 'Table of Aims' (see p. 132). On the basis of these it attempts to negotiate alliances with other parties. Once an alliance has been made with a party or parties, the agreed programme of aims cannot be changed in order to make further alliances that round.

In June 1917, the parties held widely different points of view about policies. The range of views is outlined in the Table of Aims, under the following headings: the war, the land, politics and industry.

From June to November 1917, the parties were actively negotiating to gain power or strengthen their control over government.

Negotiation occurs on the basis of News Sheets. A News Sheet is read out at the beginning of each round.

Political decisions from June to November 1917 occurred against a background of rapidly changing circumstances.

News Sheet 1 describes the situation in June 1917.

News Sheet 2 shows the position in July 1917 with the start of the summer offensive and the abortive Bolshevik rising.

News Sheet 3 describes the abortive Kornilov putsch.

News Sheet 4 surveys the situation just before the Bolsheviks seized power.

Equipment

Pencils and erasers.

Procedure

1. Divide the pupils into five groups with roughly equal numbers in each.
2. When each group has decided which party it would like to represent (see Table 8.1), allocate a different party for each group as far as possible according to choice.
3. Each group then decides on a programme of aims. This programme must be checked by the teacher to ensure that it is reasonable for the group (e.g. the Bolsheviks could not reasonably include in their programme A.1. from the Table of Aims).
4. A News Sheet is read out.
5. A time limit for negotiation is set, and negotiation between groups begins.
6. At the end of the negotiating session, the system of scoring must be carefully gone through and each group's Score Table quickly checked for correctness.
7. Continue with Rounds 2 and 3 as above.

The Russian Revolution

The Russian Revolution is a game designed to show what it was like to be caught up in the events of March to November 1917 in Russia. Each group of players will take the role of one of the following:

1. The Bolsheviks
2. The Liberals
3. The Army commanders
4. The Petrograd workers, the Kronstadt sailors and the ex-soldiers of Petrograd
5. The Mensheviks and the Social Revolutionaries

The object of the game is to make an alliance with other parties to form a government around an agreed set of *aims*. The programme is chosen from the Table of Aims provided (see p. 132). The group of players which has made the most realistic alliance with other parties will be the winner.

The game lasts for three rounds. Read the following instructions through before you start. *If you do this thoroughly you will have a much better chance of winning,* i.e. forming a government with a realistic programme.

Round 1

(a)   The controller will lay down the time for the round.

(b)   Read the document 'Parties in June 1917' (on pp. 134 – 135.) and then fill in the table below. For each point, give a mark out of 5. If you think a party is strong on a point, give it high marks, e.g. 4 or 5 out of 5. If you think it is weak, give it low marks, e.g. 0 or 1 out of 5.

Arrange the parties in order of preference, the party with the most marks being first. It may be possible for you to take the role of the party of your first choice; if not, the controller will allow you your second or third choice.

(c)   When the controller has agreed on your role, one of the *News Sheets* (see p.136) will be read out. Combine this information with what you know already, and choose *four* aims from the Table of Aims (p. 132) which you think will be best suited to

Table 8.1

Points	Parties				
	BOLSHEVIKS	LIBERALS	ARMY COMMANDERS	PETROGRAD WORKERS	MENSHEVIKS
Great military strength					
Well organized					
Support of the workers					
Realistic programme					
Appeal to other parties					
Totals					

your party. Choose *one* aim from each heading: *A*. The War; *B*. The Land; *C*. Politics; *D*. Industry. Indicate the aims chosen by writing their numbers in the spaces below.

Section	A	B	C	D
Number of aim				

(d) Submit your list of aims to the controller. If your list is approved, you can now begin to negotiate with other parties to form an alliance. If your list is unrealistic it will not be approved and your party may not begin negotiations. You must reconsider your choice of aims. Submit your altered list: if it is accepted, you may negotiate. If it is again rejected, repeat the procedure.

(e) On the basis of your aims and the situation revealed by the News Sheet, you can now negotiate with one or more parties to form an alliance around an agreed programme of four aims, one drawn from each of the four sections. In order to reach agreement with another party you may have to change your aims. When you have agreed upon a programme, indicate the party or parties you have reached agreement with, and the aims you have agreed to support in the table below. If you have made agreements with more than one party, there must still be a *single* common programme of aims.

Party/parties allied with

Section	A	B	C	D
Number of aim				

(f) Scoring: this occurs at the end of each round.

1. Before a side can score, it must ally itself with one or more parties.

2. To score: using the score table below:

(a) In column 1 write the numbers of the aims first agreed upon.

(b) In column 2 write the numbers of the common aims agreed on with the other party/parties.

(c) In column 3 write the difference between these numbers. Then add up this column, and write the result opposite 'Total'.

(d) If an alliance has been made with two or more parties, write the following figures in the 'Alliance' section:

4 for alliance with two other parties.

8 for alliance with three other parties.

12 for alliance with four other parties.

(e) *Subtract* the 'Alliance' figure from 'Total' and place the result opposite 'Final total'. This figure may be minus.

3. Transfer the figure from 'Final total' to 'Score for Round 1' of the Results table on p. 132. If *no* alliance has been made, write the figure 16 in this space.

Score table – Round 1

Column 1	Column 2	Column 3
A	A	
B	B	
C	C	
D	D	
Total		
Alliance		
Final total		

Round 2

(a) At the start of this round another News Sheet will be read out or announced. This will show changes in the situation.

(b) On the basis of your aims at the end of Round 1 and the situation which the latest News Sheet has revealed, revise what you think your aims should be. List them below.

Section	A	B	C	D
Number of aim				

(c) Submit your new list of aims to the controller. If your list is approved, you can begin to negotiate for a new set of allies, regardless of whom you allied with in Round 1. If not, follow the procedure laid down in Rule (c), Round 1.

(d) On the basis of your aims and the situation revealed by the News Sheet, you can negotiate with other parties to form an alliance around an agreed programme of aims. In order to reach agreement with another party, you may have to change your aims. When you have reached agreement upon a programme, indicate the parties you have allied with and the aims you have agreed to support in the spaces below.

Party/parties allied with

Section	A	B	C	D
Number of aim				

(e) Scoring is as in Round 1.

Score table – Round 2

Column 1	Column 2	Column 3
A	A	
B	B	
C	C	
D	D	
Total		
Alliance		
Final total		

Round 3

(a) Rules as for Round 2.

(b) State *aims* below:

Section	A	B	C	D
Number of aim				

(c) State alliance(s) and agreed aims below:

Party/parties allied with

Section	A	B	C	D
Number of aim				

(d) Scoring as in Rounds 1 and 2.

Score table – Round 3

Column 1	Column 2	Column 3
A	A	
B	B	
C	C	
D	D	
Total		
Alliance		
Final total		

Results table

Round	Score
1	
2	
3	

Table of Aims

Section A: The war

1. You are in favour of a full-scale attack on the German armies to turn defeat into victory.
2. You support a defensive war, hoping that the Allies will defeat the Germans in the west.

3. You are in favour of peace with Germany, but refuse to surrender any Russian territory.
4. You are in favour of peace at any price, and you will be prepared to surrender very large areas of Russian territory if necessary.

Section B: The land

1. You support the land policy the government laid down before 1914. This allowed the wealthier peasants to buy their farms from the estate owners.
2. You would buy the aristocrats' estates and give these to the peasants.
3. You would confiscate the aristocrats' estates, and give these to the peasants.
4. You are in favour of complete state ownership of the land, with the government running all farms.

Section C: Politics

1. You wish to create a government which represents the property owners of Russia — the merchants, factory owners, landed aristocracy, gentry etc.
2. You desire a popularly elected *duma* (a parliament based on the professional classes) which will choose a government.
3. You want complete workers' control over the government through their popularly elected assemblies (*soviets*). These will gain power through *duma* elections.
4. You favour violent revolution. You are willing to use a private army to overthrow the government.

Section D: Industry

1. You would continue the present system of private ownership, with some government support.
2. You would back the government takeover of key war industries. These would be sold to private buyers at the end of the war.
3. You think the government should have full control over industry, while allowing most of it to remain in private hands.
4. You want complete workers' control over all factories, which will be owned by the state.

133

Parties in June 1917

The Liberals

They took over the government in March 1917, after the overthrow of the Tsar. Kerensky, a thirty-six-year-old lawyer and former Minister of War, has emerged as Prime Minister after the Liberal government was set up. Kerensky is a member of the Petrograd Soviet, the body which represents the workers and soldiers in Petrograd. As the rest of the government is formed mainly from business and professional men, Kerensky is in a strong position. He has the backing of most of the officers in the Army, as well as the industrialists. The government is committed to a programme of fighting the war more efficiently, and it gained power on these grounds. At present it is actively preparing to embark on a summer offensive against the Germans. In the countryside, the government has not supported the peasants' demands to take over the land. In the towns, the factory workers are unhappy at the long hours they are still expected to work.

The Army Commanders

Their leader is General Kornilov, who supports Kerensky. The Army officers continue the tradition of the Tsarist regime and are determined to push the war against the Germans to a successful conclusion. However, they are very worried about the state of the Army, as there has been widespread desertion among the soldiers. This is because Bolshevik propaganda has stirred up a feeling of revulsion against the officers and the war. The officers support a strong, efficient and authoritarian form of government. Increasingly, they are concerned with the situation in the major cities, Petrograd and Moscow, and in the countryside where a great number of estates have already been taken over by the peasants.

The Petrograd Workers

They are in an unsettled mood. They are represented in the Petrograd Soviet and are already pressing for an end to the war. Their main area of power is in the working-class districts, where low wages and rising prices have caused unrest. The workers favour the idea of the government taking over industry. A major element in their ranks are the soldiers who have deserted from the front, and who have been influenced by socialist preaching. In the March Revolution, the soldiers played an important part and were joined by the Tsarist garrison. At nearby Kronstadt, the sailors are an important revolutionary element, ready to rebel against their officers and support any party which will meet their demands.

The Mensheviks and Social Revolutionaries

They are the two most powerful revolutionary parties, and they dominate the Petrograd Soviet. The Social Revolutionaries support the policy of sharing out the land of the great estate owners among the peasants. Originally they supported the war and Kerensky was one of their leaders, but they have become increasingly pacifist. The other group, the Mensheviks, is based on the cities and it is the most important party in the Soviet. They back a programme of state ownership of industry and of the land. They are committed to a popularly elected and democratic government. A problem of the Mensheviks is that they do not have a strong leader, and they oppose the use of force.

The Bolsheviks

Their leader is Lenin and they believe in the same programme as the Mensheviks, but they are much more interested in seizing power through armed revolution. Although they are few in number, they are extremely well organized. With Trotsky in charge of their military affairs they can clearly pose a major threat through enrolling ex-soldiers in Petrograd and sailors at Kronstadt. Already they are forming their own private army, the Red Guard. However, they have one major disadvantage; namely that their leaders returned to Russia after a long period of exile. The German government sent these leaders back to cause trouble and weaken the Russian war effort. The question of whether they are German agents has made the other parties suspicious of them. Since returning, Lenin has been busy organizing the Bolsheviks and promoting the slogans of 'Peace, bread and land' and 'Power to the soviets'.

News Sheets

News Sheet 1

The situation in the Russian capital, Petrograd, is very tense. The war is going badly, but the Liberal government under Kerensky is about to launch a major offensive against the Germans. Kerensky has just returned from the front, where he has been visiting the troops to encourage them to make a final effort for victory. In Moscow he has rallied the industrialists, bankers and professional men to support the campaign. However, in Petrograd he is faced with the powerful opposition of the Bolsheviks: they have only a small minority in the Soviet, but there are 50,000 men in their party and they have close ties with the sailors at Kronstadt. In the countryside, with the encouragement of the Social Revolutionaries, the peasants are still taking over the estates of the great landowners.

News Sheet 2

The campaign against the Germans has got off to a flying start. Support has rallied to Kerensky and the government. The Austrian and German forces have been thrown back about 96 kilometres. However, the Bolsheviks have seized upon the existing war-weariness of the ex-soldiers in Petrograd and the sailors at Kronstadt and have mounted a mass demonstration against the government. A large force of Kronstadt sailors, claiming to support the Bolsheviks, has marched on the headquarters of the government. The situation is confused, but it seems that a large number of Bolsheviks have joined the sailors. Lenin and the other Bolshevik leaders have claimed that they have nothing to do with the rising. News has arrived that the government forces have the situation under control and have routed the demonstrators.

Clearly there has been a botched attempt at a rising in Petrograd. Otherwise the situation is relatively unchanged. Industry is still working flat out, with the Mensheviks and Social Revolutionaries sticking to their programme. Kerensky seems as determined as ever to push the war programme, but in domestic affairs he seems to have little hope of stopping the peasant takeover of the land. Although the Social Revolutionaries and the Mensheviks are in favour of peace, they do not want to be accused of breaking Russia's alliance with Britain and France.

News Sheet 3

News has been received of major Allied reverses on the Western Front. Large numbers of Russian deserters have entered Petrograd and swelled the numbers of unemployed. With rising prices and no wage increases, the workers are in an ugly mood. There are reports that the Army commander, General Kornilov, has decided to march on Petrograd and take over the government. Relations between him and Kerensky have been strained for some time, although there are rumours that Kerensky intends to support a military takeover. Information has just arrived that Kornilov is definitely moving his troops towards the capital. If this is true, it could mean the end of the revolutionary movement. The Mensheviks and Social Revolutionaries are still opposed to any attempts to force the government's hand, because they do not believe that it is time for the working class to take power. The Bolsheviks claim that Kerensky has asked for their help against Kornilov. They have organized their military support into an army, the Red Guard. The government has completely lost control over the countryside, where the Social Revolutionaries are dominant. Only the Bolsheviks are backing a move for peace at any price, although the Petrograd workers would be willing to see an end to the war, and a return to peace and industrial prosperity.

New Sheet 4

Since the failure of Kornilov's rising, and his arrest, the Army commanders have been hostile to Kerensky. The refusal of their forces to support Kornilov means that they are in a very weak position, although still committed to the war. Kerensky is desperately searching for support after the complete failure of the war effort and the approach of the German armies towards Moscow. In Petrograd, the workers' conditions have become much worse, and the Bolsheviks are encouraging them to oppose the government and push for a peace agreement. Industry is declining fast as the government collapses. Petrograd is virtually isolated from the rest of Russia, and the sailors of Kronstadt seem to be preparing to rise against the government. They are in close touch with the Bolsheviks. The

137

Mensheviks still support constitutional government, and are opposed to the use of force.

Role Table

Take the role allocated to you. The numbers refer to the number of players in each group.

The Bolsheviks

1. Lenin
2. Trotsky
3. Krupskaya, Lenin's wife
4. Stalin, editor of *Pravda*
5. Member of the Petrograd Soviet
6. Leader of the Kronstadt sailors
7. Leader of a group of deserters and a member of the Red Guard
8. Petrograd worker and a member of the Red Guard

The Liberals

1. Kerensky
2. Foreign minister
3. Domestic minister
4. War minister
5. Industrialist
6. Banker
7. Ex-royalist
8. Schoolmaster

The Army Commanders

1. Kornilov
2. Chief-of-Staff
3. Commander of the army at the front
4. Second-in-command of the army at the front
5. Officer from a noble family, which has lost estates to the Revolutionaries; serving at Kornilov's HQ
6. Commander of the Petrograd garrison
7. Commander of the Moscow garrison
8. Commander of the Navy

The Petrograd Workers

1. Member of the Soviet
2. Steel worker
3. Worker in a cotton mill
4. Unemployed labourer
5. Kronstadt radical
6. Kronstadt sailor
7. Ex-soldier
8. Deserter

Mensheviks and Social Revolutionaries

1. Dan, leader of the Social Revolutionaries
2. Leader of the Mensheviks
3. Menshevik member of the Soviet
4. Menshevik member of the Soviet
5. Social Revolutionary and a member of the Soviet
6. Social Revolutionary returned from helping to take over aristocrats' estates
7. Social Revolutionary returned from advising peasants on the use of their new land
8. Menshevik worker

References

Carmichael, J. *A Short History of the Russian Revolution,* Sphere, 1971.

Hasler, J. *The Making of Russia,* Longman, 1969.

Ulam, AB. *Lenin and the Bolsheviks,* Collins, 1969.

Pethybridge, R (ed). *Witnesses to the Russian Revolution,* Allen & Unwin, 1964.

Reed, JS. *Ten Days that Shook the World,* Lawrence & Wishart, 1961.

Roberts, EM. *Lenin and the Downfall of Tsarist Russia,* Methuen, 1966.

Trotsky, L. *My Life,* Thornton Butterworth, 1930.

History of the 20th Century, BPC Publishing Ltd 1968.

The Russian Revolution, Cape, (Jackdaw).

9

The Construction of History Games and Simulations

Recently there has been a considerable increase in the number of private and commercially produced history games. However, a teacher may well decide that he wishes to create his own games as the number in existence is still limited and there may be nothing suitable for a specific topic or age/ability level. The construction of games can be hard work but is enjoyable. This chapter is intended as a general guide to games' construction, pointing out the short cuts we have developed and the problems we have encountered.

Stage 1 Background

A number of things have to be borne in mind before a history simulation can be developed (these considerations soon become automatic.)

1. The *topic* must be isolated, as each game is created round a historical framework. The game should be matched to the type and complexity of the material which the pupils can handle. A major danger is overcomplexity: an enthusiastic teacher may include more and more elements in his desire to make the simulation as realistic as possible. The framework of *The Russian Revolution*,

a simulation for older pupils, is quite difficult; but even so it represents the results of ruthlessly cutting out a number of interesting factors.

2. The *type of activity* must be decided on. When starting to write games, it is best to concentrate on a single main form of activity for each simulation. Part 1 of *Ironmaster* has only one main form of gaming activity (map location), although it does contain a subsidiary decision table. With practice, the teacher will find it easy to build up compound games which combine a variety of gaming activity.

3. The precise *function* of the game in the teaching of a topic needs to be thought about. It is important to decide which aspect of the topic would most benefit from a gaming approach. Ideally, the game should enable the pupils to grasp an understanding of the event or sequence of events as they happened. The teacher must also consider at what point in the teaching programme the game should be introduced. Games tend to be highly motivating, and for this reason they make excellent introductions to a topic. They are also useful in elucidating the *processes* of history, and so may be suited to the middle of a topic, when the factual groundwork is already mastered.

4. The type of *game organization* must be considered. Assuming that a single type of gaming activity is being carried out, the simulation will involve single, group or class role-play. In making a decision, the teacher must think about the pupils who will be playing the game. Are they experienced in group work? To what extent are they self-disciplined? Are they able to move freely around the classroom without causing chaos? A general rule is: the greater the element of class role-play, the more likely organizational problems are to occur, as this form normally requires a high degree of class activity and movement, with the teacher playing a largely passive role once the simulation has been got under way.

Ironmaster, Village Enclosure and *The Development of the Medieval Town* can be played by individual pupils, pairs or small groups, although class role-play elements are included as options should the teacher wish to use them. On the other hand, *The Russian Revolution* is a class role-play demanding the total interaction of all members of a class.

Stage 2. The historical framework

The next step is the preparation of the historical material for the simulation. Since a history simulation can be used as a vehicle for presenting a great deal of accurate historical information, it pays to make use of this possibility. *Ironmaster* has been carefully based on historical records (see The game/Historical actuality on p. 66) and is more of a simulation than the commercial history game *'Diplomacy'* which only roughly approximates to the historical reality.

Two main areas of difficulty may arise in the preparation of material for a simulation.

1. Problems may be experienced in working out the form of the framework. Two factors are involved: the identification of the characters or parties involved; and the constraints on their behaviour. In *The Russian Revolution* care had to be taken to identify accurately the different parties which had emerged by June 1917 and the different programmes each supported. In *Village Enclosure* the social composition of the village had to be postulated: this was a composite picture made up mainly from local records, many of which concerned Shropshire. On this basis, 'character studies' of the squire, yeomen etc. were built up.

   Constraints in a simulation can take a physical or non-physical aspect. In *The Development of the Medieval Town* both factors are present: physical constraints occur in the siting of features (such as a new bridge); non-physical constraints modify decisions such as whether to apply for a town charter or not.

2. Simplification may be necessary. Not all the factors in a complex historical situation can be simulated, and a satisfactory framework will depend on rigorous selection of only those factors that the teacher wishes to accentuate. A further selection must take place to eliminate factors which are difficult to simulate (e.g. crowd hysteria). In group and class role-play, the number of protagonists may have to be reduced to avoid confusion (or merely for convenience). In a simulation on the Norman Conquest we decided to mention only eight great Norman barons, although in fact eleven usually attended William's *magnum consilium.* Eight enables the game to be played both as a group and a class role-play, thus giving greater flexibility to the teacher.

Stage 3. The writing of games: general factors

1. In playing a game, the pupils should be involved in some sort of action (a decision or discussion) as soon as possible. However there is often a temptation to present the pupils with a large number of rules or facts which have to be mastered before the game can begin. This can easily lead to loss of interest.

   There are various solutions. One we adopted for *Trade and Discovery*. To begin with, this game dealt with the possibilities for commercial and colonial exploitation around the year 1600. However, we found that the pupils had to master five pages of rules before they could make their first move. We therefore isolated the rules that concerned board moves and chance factors (as opposed to trading) and made up a very simple 'subgame' to familiarize the pupils with these. This subgame (shown in chapter 7) became Part 1 of our original game.

   A different solution occurs in *Frontier* and *The Russian Revolution*. Here the pupils are faced with an immediate decision as to which role they would like to take. In order to do this, they have to read a certain amount of information, but this is acceptable as they need this information to achieve a known short-term goal (the decision).

2. Vocabulary and language should be kept as simple as possible. It is all too easy to pitch the vocabulary level too high, with resulting hold-ups and misunderstandings when the simulation is played. Care needs to be taken when using technical terms (such as 'motte') that an explanation is provided, either when the term is introduced, or in a glossary.

   One of the chief problems of language is the removing of possible ambiguity: this is especially important in laying down rules for a board game or a complex class role-play. The most effective way to achieve complete clarity is to get other adults and children to read the game through; the revised draft can then be used with a small testing group before final revision for class use.

3. Equipment can pose a problem of checking and storage in the classroom, so the less a simulation needs in order to function, the better. However, in board games a number of moves often have to be taken. One solution is to have a set number of moves for each

143

turn (as in *Frontier*). Another answer is the use of a random number table. This is a piece of paper or card marked out with squares into which a 1p piece will fit. Each square is then numbered randomly, and the coin used (in much the same way as in shove-halfpenny) to determine which number is relevant for the turn. A third method is the use of a simple spinner (as on the map for *Trade and Discovery*) which can be regarded as expendable.

For dealing with chance factors, the 'chance card' (on the lines of *'Monopoly'*) seems the obvious choice. However, cards are a nuisance to cut out, and can easily get lost, so we have increasingly employed the chance *sheet* (as in *Trade and Discovery*.) This has the advantage both of doing away with cards and of allowing all the players to see what chance factors are likely to be encountered.

4. Facts and figures should as far as possible be historically accurate. However, major problems. can occur in using accurate contemporary figures for a simulation, because those figures were part of a more complex actuality than the simulation can portray. Such a problem arose in early drafts of *Ironmaster*, and it required a great deal of juggling to make the final accounting of the simulation realistic.

False figures should be avoided, however convenient they may be. In using history games, the pupils are learning by doing, and inaccurate information can easily be assimilated.

A solution is the use of 'units'. Here no actual figures are shown, but each unit is held to represent an amount of money or commodities that need not be specified (see *Frontier*.) This system works where no accurate figures are available or the data is not quantifiable. A major advantage of units is that they help avoid complicated maths and allow a simulation to be used with most ability levels.

5. Information sheets, news sheets, notes on characters etc. can contain large amounts of historical information, so they should be based where possible on actual examples, even where general patterns of behaviour are being described. If biographies are accurate and interesting, pupils will more easily be able to identify with the characters concerned. Information and news sheets are a very direct way of conveying facts on which pupils have to take

decisions and in, for example, *The Russian Revolution* they play a central part in the simulation.

The greater the historical accuracy, the greater the depth and interest of the simulation and the more the pupils will be involved in it and learn from it.

6. Historical prompts are one way of solving a major difficulty of simulation. Where the range of options open to the pupils is very wide, wildly 'unhistorical' decisions may be taken and the pupils may receive the wrong impression of what actually happened or could have happened. On the other hand, if the simulation narrowly restricts choices, the pupils may not be able to make interesting decisions.

The historical prompt returns the pupils to the historical reality after a decision or series of decisions. An example occurs at the beginning of Part 2 of *The Development of the Medieval Town*. Here Vikings are said to have destroyed site B (an unsatisfactory choice in that, among other things, it was less defensible). In Part 4 of *Ironmaster*, the pupils are informed that by 1790 coke blast furnaces were established, although for the first three parts (set in 1760) the pupils may have chosen charcoal furnaces.

Another way of restricting the effects of unlikely choices is for the teacher to assess the results of decisions, giving high marks for 'historical probability'. Alternatively, he can refuse to accept an improbable choice, as in *The Russian Revolution* where each party has to have its programme passed by the teacher before it can begin to negotiate.

7. Chance factors in a simulation give some idea of the part chance plays in history. For the gaming point of view chance cards or sheets are useful as they introduce variety and interest. They should not be too uniformly pessimistic or they will tend to discourage some players. However, it is a good idea to have one chance factor which will completely reverse the fortunes of a player: in this way a 'winning' player can never feel safe and bored, and a 'losing' player always has the hope of good fortune.

As with the framework, chance cards/sheets should be as historically accurate as possible. An example of how this can be done is shown in The game/Historical actuality for chapter 7.

Stage 4. *The writing of games: specific game elements*

In dealing with certain types of game activity, the following pointers may be helpful:

1. *Board games – reality.* The board can either be divided up into areas (squares etc.) or be marked with routes which have to be followed (see an early version of *Trade and Discovery* in *Teaching History,* May 1972, vol. 2, no. 8). The latter method makes the simulation much easier to construct as there are fewer variables. If squares are being used, it is advisable to make these quite large: this makes for simplification and leaves no doubt which square a player's piece is in.

   To speed up the game, chance cards and wind arrows (or their equivalents) can be used, as in *Trade and Discovery.*

2. *Board game – abstraction.* The board should be divided up into equal-sized areas, with each area denoting the same period of time. (A game on the Reform Bill, covering 1830-32, might have thirty-six squares each representing a month.) It is advisable to restrict the 'jumps' players can make, or they may miss out vital stages in chronological development. For the same reason, players should not be allowed to go back on the board or their view of the event may become muddled; if a penalty is required, it should be to stop on the square they have reached.

3. *Map game – location exercise.* The map should show sufficient topographical factors for a thoughtful decision to be made about sites, routes, positioning of features etc. Such a decision should be between valid alternatives, but may include a possible choice that is definitely wrong, e.g. in Part 1 of *The Development of the Medieval Town* where sites A and C are equally valid, but site B is definitely unsuitable. This 'unsuitable' element is designed to show the pupils that although there may not be any uniquely 'right' answer, a thoughtless choice may be definitely wrong. This discourages guessing.

4. *Map game – development.* The map should be divided into areas. We like to use squares as they are easy to draw, and some other shapes (hexagons, for instance) tend to make the map appear cluttered. Each square should cover an area which can be exploited, settled or occupied during a specific period of time, or according

146

to rules laid down. *Frontier* is typical of a game where settlement occurs; Part 3 of *Village Enclosure* shows the occupation of holdings according to certain constraints. Such constraints should be as historically accurate as possible.

5. *Map game – progression.* The difficulty with this form is that it is totally open-ended: an outline map has to be filled in with various features in any way that seems reasonable to the pupils. The rules and procedures have, therefore, to be rigorous, cutting out the possibilities for unreasonable sitings and so on. It is a good idea to include illustrative examples of the size and type of features before they go onto the map (see *The Development of the Medieval Town*): this prevents distortions of scale.

6. *Tables – decision, analysis, account.* In laying these out, it is recommended that the number of factors to be numerically assessed is limited to five. The 'marking' of the factors is normally out of 5 or 10. Where the 'points for' and the 'points against' a series of factors or line of action are being assessed, it is essential to *split* the decision and have one table 'for' and a separate one 'against'. If this is not done, considerable confusion can result, particularly with younger pupils.

7. *Discussion – negotiation.* Where a group or class role-play negotiation game is being written, the following procedure may be helpful:

(a) The characters should be delineated, and the method by which the pupils choose such characters stated (by allocation on the part of the teacher, or by some form of pupils' choice).

(b) When roles have been taken, the players will have to outline a coherent programme of aims. A check can be built into the game, with the teacher able to accept/reject a proposed programme before negotiation with other pupils takes place.

(c) The method of negotiation, and the consequences of any alliances or deals must be clearly outlined.

(d) Details of scoring, or other ways of achieving a result, should be made clear.

(e) A time limit should be set.

8. *Discussion – debate.* It is advisable to lay down a strict order of speaking (as in *Village Enclosure* Part 2, Table 6.4). This encourages the shy pupils to say something, and prevents the more forceful or fluent from dominating proceedings.

9. *In/out tray – linear.* The function of the in/out tray method is to show historical change taking place during the course of a simulation. As the name implies, information is presented to the pupil (put in his 'In' tray), digested by him and acted on (his directions for action would go in an 'Out' tray). The key to using this method is that any historical information presented should always be *used* by the pupil in making decisions.

   The linear form is suitable for the simulation covering a long period of time, e.g. *The Development of the Medieval Town* which deals with a period of some seven centuries. In constructing such a 'line of development' simulation, it is best to divide it up into separate parts (normally up to six), which will each take one period to play through. A part can show a particular stage in development, and can be introduced by an in/out tray element which will lay down certain constraints for that part (e.g. Part 3 of *The Development of the Medieval Town* states that the Norman Conquest has taken place: this modifies the form of the town).

10. *In/out tray – complex.* In this, the pupils are given news/information sheets at specific points in the negotiation sessions. The information changes the situation within which negotiation is carried on. The important thing to achieve is a major change in the circumstances which affect group decisions. However, a difficulty arises when the information is historically accurate and the pupils may know the sequence of events or their outcome. A solution is to take an actual situation but use fictitious names and dates - although this may produce problems in transferring from the simulation back to the historical reality after the game.

   If the game sticks to historical reality, we have found the best solutions are as follows:

   (a) Provide news sheets in chronological order, but in far greater number than will be used (e.g. ten news sheets might be written down in the text, but only three of these read out during the course of the simulation). Pupils will then not be able to modify their actions to take advantage of future events: for instance, in *The Russian Revolution* it may be unwise to make an alliance with the Bolsheviks (although they eventually triumphed) because the news sheets concerning their failed putsch may be read out.

(b) Provide news sheets in random order in the text, but read them out in chronological order during the game. The disadvantage of this solution is that clever pupils soon are able to predict which news sheet is coming next.

We hope the above will be helpful in two ways: it should aid *analysis* of existing simulations and help in choosing ones suitable for a teacher's particular needs; and it should make the *construction* of simulations easier. With regard to the second, we are acutely aware that all the procedures outlined here may appear intimidating. The reason we have included them is that they represent short cuts: simulation is a time consuming activity, and although we have enjoyed constructing such material we could have saved hours if initially we had had a list of procedures to work from.

The great thing is: have a go, beginning with something simple. If the worst happens, and the simulation fails to demonstrate what it was meant to, the pupils will eagerly compare it with the historical reality – and thus learn history.

10
History Games and Simulations in the Classroom

Having written a game, the teacher looks forward to trying it out and seeing if it fulfils expectations. Normally we have found that games have gone better than we had a right to expect. Even where elements have not been completely clear, the result has often been an interesting discussion of factors which might otherwise have been glossed over. However, as with any other teaching aid, one should aim for the best possible presentation and organization, and the following general guidelines and specific points should be of help.

There are three stages in using a simulation: introduction, play through and follow up.

Introduction

How much preparatory work is necessary depends on the nature of the simulation. We try to make our simulations as self-contained as possible so that they can be introduced into a course with the minimum of preparation. But there is no reason why a simulation should not be exploratory, i.e. one that will impel the pupils to find out about the topic in order to play successfully.

The teacher will have to decide when to introduce the simulation into a course. It could be used as a stimulating introduction to a topic; alternatively, a simulation might occur in the middle of a topic to illustrate aspects not covered by textbooks or available books of reference.

Play-through

Specific points about the playing of games are dealt with under seven headings:

1. Reading the text

Where possible, pupils should read the text aloud to ensure that the whole class takes it in. It pays to stop the reading at certain points to ask questions: this will reveal if the pupils fully understand the game. Such questions should be encouraged; one of the problems of writing games is that while they seem perfectly explicit to the author, they may not be clear to the pupils.

2. Working through tables

All decision, analysis and account tables should be clearly explained and examples worked through on a class basis before pupils attempt to fill them in by themselves. One method of doing this is to introduce a 'class decision' element into tables, particularly those occurring early in a game (see Part 1 of *Ironmaster* and *Village Enclosure*). This works as follows. When the table has been explained and all the points and factors examined, the pupils assess *one* point for *one* factor (e.g. in *Village Enclosure* Site A, Point 1 in Table 6.1). Each pupil/group then states how many marks out of 10 it has given and the mark with the largest number of supporters is entered under 'Class result'. Any wide discrepancies of marking can then be discussed and misunderstandings put right. With younger or less able pupils it may be necessary to work through several 'Class results'.

A further function of the class decision occurs when all pupils have completed a table. The remainder of the 'Class result' columns can then be filled in and the total class results compared with individual total results.

3. Organizing pupils

In single role-plays we usually have the pupils working in pairs, with pupils of different ability working together.

In group role-plays we have found it best to restrict the number of pupils to four per group. This is particularly important where the pupils are taking turns to make moves: with larger numbers, interest tends to fade if there is a large time lag between moves. If the game does not have a system for allocating roles the teacher should do this, perhaps in alphabetical order.

Class role-plays need careful organization. It is normally best first to divide the class into groups representing different parties or characters, and then allow the pupils within each group to decide on individual roles.

If the pupils are unfamiliar with negotiation, initial sessions should be kept short and problems dealt with as they arise.

4. Timing

The timing of a game needs to be carefully watched. By sticking to a schedule, the pupils gain a sense of urgency and try hard to achieve their objects within the time limit. This is particularly true of games with a competitive element. In a compound game, it helps if each new part can coincide with the beginning of a lesson, especially when pupils take different roles in different parts (as in *The Development of the Medieval Town and Village Enclosures*).

5. Equipment

This should be reduced to a minimum. Anything needed (spinners, dice, pieces or cards) should be prepared before the start of a simulation, either by the teacher or the pupils, who should also be warned if pencils and erasers will be required. These steps help avoid confusion at the start of a game.

6. Problems

These can occur in competitive games if the question of cheating arises, leading to the pupils arguing about non-historical factors. Such a problem may occur during group or class role-plays, so when using these types of simulation the teacher should make sure that he can be free to join any group in which trouble arises to solve the problem.

A second source of potential problems is where a section of a game has to be completed by each pair or group before the class can move on to the next element (as in *Village Enclosure*). In this case

152

groups which work faster than the rest should have ancillary material to work on during pauses. Such material might be a text book or the writing up of a diary of their character's activities during the game.

Thirdly, a pupil may make an improbable decision which he then stoutly defends. This potential problem can be turned to good use by involving the class in a discussion of the soundness of the decision in relation to the historical framework. This makes for excellent practice in the use of historical evidence.

7. *Completing the game*

Some games have a competitive element and end with one player or group being the winner. In *Ironmaster* the firm which makes the most profit wins, while in *Trade and Discovery* the player who first sails round the world is the victor. However, with simulations such as *Village Enclosure* and *The Development of the Medieval Town* there are no 'winners' as such, but the teacher may wish to evaluate the finished maps, tables or diaries.

Follow-up

Follow-up is important: it may largely consist of class discussion about the game and its overall impact. Such discussion helps strengthen the long-term recall of the pupils, and can cover some of the following points:

(a) The relation between the simulation and the historical actuality.
(b) A comparison between individual and class decisions, covering the whole range of negotiations, debates, tables, maps etc.
(c) The amount of information the pupils have absorbed about the topic. Particular attention can be paid to whether they have a grasp of the concepts which underlie the historical framework.
(d) What has been absorbed about the interaction of individuals and groups in history, and the way in which people in the past arrived at decisions.

The follow-up can also include written work. If a journal has been kept during the game, it can be expanded. Events can be portrayed in the form of letters from the characters concerned, or as newspaper accounts. Alternatively, oral or dramatic work can be attempted, including taped commentaries or interviews and scripted or unscripted plays.

An account of a particular game in action may help make the points above clearer; the following shows a play-through of *Village Enclosure* with a class of fourteen-year-old boys of slightly above average ability. The game was introduced at a point in the syllabus where changes in agricultural technology and the breeding of live-stock had been dealt with, so the pupils were acquainted with some aspects of the background against which the enclosure movement occurred.

Texts were prepared for each of the thirty pupils and ancillary material collected. This included two textbooks (RJ Cootes; *Britain since 1700,* and AJ Patrick; *The Making of a Nation 1603-1789*), atlases and a wall display on agricultural changes. Also at hand were two filmstrips on the Agricultural Revolution (Common Ground: 'Agriculture and the Land', 1 and 2), so that points could be visually illustrated as they arose.

Period 1

The pupils had been told that they would be working through a simulation so they arrived in a state of expectation as several did not know what this was. They had been asked to bring pencils: inevitably, some forgot, and so for future periods a reserve supply of pencils and erasers was kept in the classroom.

The pupils divided into pairs and work on Part 1 began straight away. The text was read out, with no pupil reading more than a sen-tence, and the teacher put in the occasional question to make certain that terms such as 'squire' were understood in their early nineteenth-century context. The three sites on Map 1 were examined and various points discussed; for instance, was it possible to cross the river from Site C to reach the common?

After discussion, Table 6.1 was attempted, using the procedure out-lined in Section 2 on p. 151. This was the first decision table that some of the class had filled in, so it took about fifteen minutes, slightly longer than anticipated. The 'Class result' for the table was that Site B was selected, but two pairs decided on Site C and this generated interesting discussion.

154

The purpose of Part 1 had largely been to introduce the pupils to gaming and to set the scene for the main body of the simulation. The pupils had now:

(a) Been introduced to the decision-making process.
(b) Learnt how to use tables.
(c) Become used to working in cooperation with other pupils.
(d) Gained some practice in classroom discussion.

Period 2

After a brief resumé of Part 1, the text of Part 2 was read aloud down to 'The Enclosure decision'. The pupils then read the notes on 'Village characters' for themselves, and each pair decided which character it would like to represent. The teacher then read down the list in Table 6.2 and allocated roles as far as possible according to choice. The fifteenth pair took the role of a squatter family. (In later plays through of the simulation, it was found more satisfactory to enlarge the fourteenth groups if there were more than twenty-eight in a class, as the squatters do not have a vote in Part 3, Table 6.4.)

The section beginning 'The enclosure decision' was read aloud down to Point F of Table 6.3. Each pair then tried to decide what was its attitude to enclosure. After this, there was a brief negotiating session during which the pupils circulated fo find out what other landowners thought, attempting to persuade them if they held contrary views.

Each pair was told that it would have to prepare a case for the next lesson's debate, and decide which one of the pair was going to present it.

Period 3

Pupils who had remembered to work out their speech arrived full of anticipation, with some flourishing impressive looking notes. Arguments were already under way before the lesson began, so the teacher stated that he was the parish constable and would conduct the meeting in an orderly and formal fashion. One of the squatters expressed doubts about his capacity to do this.

The debate then began, with characters speaking in the order set out in Table 6.4. There was a surprising variety in approach: some

155

speakers were quite subtle, attempting to hide the interests which their biographies stated; others were blunt and even threatening, others abusive. Several of the Small Freeholders appealed to the good nature of the Rector, realizing that he could swing the decision. As each speaker finished, and declared himself either for or against enclosure, his decision was marked down in Table 6.4.

The decision of the village was *not* to enclose, largely owing to the spirited pleas of two of the Freeholders. It had been intended to have a further negotiating session during which pressure could be brought on waverers to reverse or uphold the decision of the meeting, but the debate took all the time available.

Period 4

The beginning of Part 3 caused some annoyance, since it reversed the previous decision of the class. Most of the pupils eventually agreed that the point was historically valid, but a small vociferous group formed an antiprogress lobby and showed grave displeasure with what was happening to their village. This interesting and promising discussion had to be cut short owing to time difficulties.

There was also a little difficulty with the change of role to that of Enclosure Commissioners, as some pairs had identified strongly with their previous roles. (In retrospect, it might have been better to form new pairs for this Part: this should have made it easier to get across the idea that as Commissioners the pupils *had* to be socially biased.)

After these contretemps, the map progression exercise (Map 9, The results of enclosure) went well and the allocation of the new fields was soon completed. This is a very open-ended exercise, and there was a good deal of subdued discussion within each pair.

Pairs then exchanged maps and worked through the analysis table (Table 6.6). This revealed that almost all the pupils had allocated land realistically.

Period 5

The class was warned that Part 5 is the most difficult section of the simulation, so pairs approached it carefully. There was no difficulty in deciding who bought the land of the Small Freeholders, nor with

156

the transference of the new field pattern from Map 8 to Map 9. Finally the new farms and tracks were drawn in.

The pupils formed groups of four, each pair discussing differences between its maps and those of the other pair. The groups then exchanged maps for wider comparison.

Period 6

The first half of this period was taken up with a general discussion about the simulation, which was compared to the two standard textbooks, filmstrips and wall display. There was a lively examination of how typical the Rector was: many pupils thought that such a figure would have been more at home in the mid-eighteenth century. Also, the 2½ inch maps of the area round the school were got out to see how far these conformed to Map 9.

The pupils then began to write an account of the whole enclosure procedure, from the point of view of any one of the villagers. This was completed in time provided out of class, and some perceptive accounts resulted.

The pupils seemed enthusiastic about the method, and although some snags had arisen, the impetus generated by the game carried the class over these. The long-term results were also encouraging: in the exam a large number of the pupils opted for the enclosure question and showed that they had both absorbed a large amount of information and realized its significance.

Longman History Games

The games listed below, reproduce the main features of original situations and allow pupils to react to problems faced by individuals and groups in history. In this way, pupils experience history *from the inside* and are motivated by the roles they take. Decisions based on evaluation of evidence and negotiation deepen understanding of historical facts and processes.

Practising teachers have written the games and tested them widely. Trials have been conducted with a range of ability and age level (11-18 years). The games have been modified through teacher and pupil comment and by criticism resulting from articles in the *T.E.S.* and *Teaching History.*

HISTORY GAMES — TEACHERS' UNIT

Opens with a brief introduction to the educational use of simulations and games and an outline of the development of the materials published through this scheme.

The main content is a series of Teachers' Notes giving the aims of each game, practical suggestions for class organisation, playing procedures and the background knowledge required by pupils. The notes also make recommendations for the selection of sections within a game to suit various age and ability levels and give estimates of the time required to complete each stage.

THE SUBSCRIPTION SCHEME

The History Games subscription scheme offers a collection of games which are flexible in use and suit most syllabuses and teaching methods. They span 400 AD to 1926 and although the accent is primarily on British history, games on North America and Africa are included. Each game contains illustrations and documentary material.

The educational value of the gaming technique has been widely accepted but its use has been limited by the high cost of game sets. The History Games subscription scheme narrows the gap between classroom needs and the department budget by offering a substantial quantity of material at a low unit price.

The games are available through a subscription scheme under which you can obtain your choice of title and quantity for up to a total of 90 History Games units for pupil use, and a complete reference set of the Teacher's Unit and one copy of each game. For details of the subscription scheme, please write to: The Publishing Manager,
Longman Group Limited — Resources Unit,
35 Tanner Row,
York.

HISTORY GAMES

THE NORMAN CONQUEST D. Birt and J. Nichol, **THE DEVELOPMENT OF THE MEDIEVAL TOWN** D. Birt and J. Nichol, **FRONTIER** D. Birt and J. Nichol, **TRADE AND DISCOVERY** D. Birt and J. Nichol, **IRONMASTER** D. Birt and J. Nichol, **CANALS** B. Barker and R. Boden, **VILLAGE ENCLOSURE** D. Birt and J. Nichol, **CONGRESS OF VIENNA** B. Barker and R. Boden, **HARVEST POLITICS** B. Barker and R. Boden, **RAILWAY MANIA** B. Barker and R. Boden, **THE SCRAMBLE FOR AFRICA** B. Barker and R. Boden, **GENERAL STRIKE** B. Barker and R. Boden.